EMPERORS OF ROME

THE MONSTERS

FROM TIBERIUS TO THEODORA, AD 14–548

PAUL CHRYSTAL

Pen & Sword
MILITARY

First published in Great Britain in 2018 by
PEN AND SWORD MILITARY
an imprint of
Pen and Sword Books Ltd
47 Church Street
Barnsley
South Yorkshire S70 2AS

Copyright © Paul Chrystal, 2018

ISBN 978 1 52672 885 2

Typeset by Aura Technology and Software Services, India
Printed and bound by CPI Group (UK) Ltd, Croydon, CR0 4YY

Pen & Sword Books Ltd incorporates the imprints of Pen & Sword
Archaeology, Atlas, Aviation, Battleground, Discovery, Family History, History, Maritime, Military,
Naval, Politics, Railways, Select, Social History, Transport, True Crime, Claymore Press, Frontline
Books, Leo Cooper, Praetorian Press, Remember When, Seaforth Publishing and Wharncliffe.

For a complete list of Pen and Sword titles please contact
Pen and Sword Books Limited
47 Church Street, Barnsley, South Yorkshire, S70 2AS, England
email: enquiries@pen-and-sword.co.uk
website: www.pen-and-sword.co.uk

CONTENTS

The Roman Empire, AD 210. (Mandrak/Cristiano64)

INTRODUCTION

This book is part of the Pen & Sword series on history's architects of terror, books which are designed to describe the repellent nature and actions of the monsters who have stained world history down the years. *The Shorter Oxford English Dictionary* defines monster in this context as "a person of inhuman cruelty or wickedness" and monstrous as "deviating from the natural order, atrocious, horrible".

There are certainly a number of Roman emperors, and empresses, who merit the description 'monster', as this book will show; however, it is not the intention or purpose to offer yet another sensational and salacious catalogue of imperial deviants. Rather, the unnatural actions and atrocities of these emperors will be described, as far as possible, in the context of their times, the contemporary politics and societal norms. This is not an attempt to mitigate in any way their actions or to apologize for their bestial behaviour, simply to provide, as far as possible, balanced accounts given that some of the primary sources we rely on—Suetonius's *Lives of the Caesars* and the *Historia Augusta* for example—are often infected with prejudice and a hankering after the sensationally tabloid. Moreover it is important that we never forget: Hitler and Stalin, monsters both, argued smugly that no one remembers the Ottoman government's industrial extermination of 1.5 million Armenians from April 1915 or the sack of Novgorod by Tsar Ivan IV 'The Formidable' in 1570. Books such as this will ensure that we do remember and that we do not forget. Only by not forgetting do we have the slimmest of chances to learn from the abominations and their perpetrators and perhaps avert some future outrages. At the same time, we should be alert to the fact that the many victims—real people—suffered torture, extreme fear and anxiety and, often, a painful death—their only crime was being in the wrong place at the wrong time, and subjected to the whim of a deranged monster. It is important that the list of abominations described here does not become just that—a list.

As with everything else, there were good and bad Roman emperors and empresses. The good, like Trajan (98–117), Hadrian (117–138), Antoninus Pius (138–161), and Marcus Aurelius (161–180) were largely civilized and civilizing. The bad, on the other hand, exhibited varying degrees of corruption, cruelty, depravity and insanity. It is sobering to remember that these brutes were responsible for governing the greatest civilization in the world despite their terror and brutality and massacres.

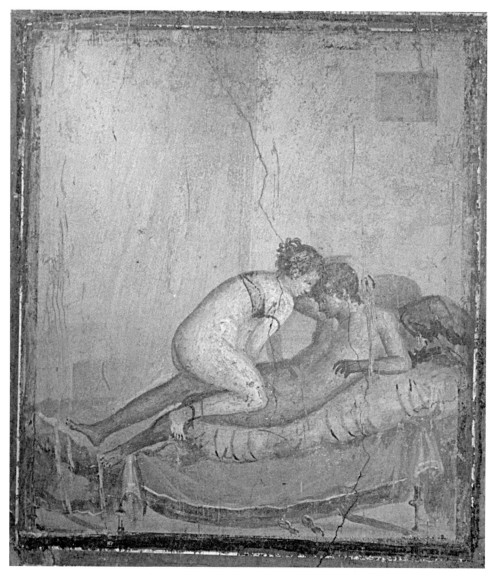

An explicit mural from Pompeii—unlikely to have raised many eyebrows.

Tiberius, Caligula, Nero, Domitian, Commodus, Caracalla, Elagabalus, Septimius Severus, Diocletian, Justinian, Theodora and the rest all had more bad days than good. Their exploits have, of course, been well documented since classical times but much of the coverage can only be called gratuitous, sensationalist or tabloid, published with an eye on sales rather than the facts. This book is based on primary sources and

Roman decadence contributed ultimately to its destruction, an 1836 painting by Thomas Cole.

evidence—and it attempts to balance out, though not excuse, the shocking with any mitigating aspects in each of the lives.

Part of the reason for the sensationalism is, of course, the unreliability of the sources. Tacitus—perhaps the most balanced and most contemporary, is nevertheless guilty of political bias against Nero and Domitian, for example. The biographer Suetonius in his twelve lives, was writing some time after his subjects' lives and unashamedly spiced up his biographies with a selective approach to his own sources in order to satisfy his need for a racy, sensationalist account of each of the emperors. The *Historia Augusta* and its authors were even less troubled by the truth or the facts if they got in the way of a good story—more selectivity but padded out with false facts and fantasy. It is important as well to apply a certain degree of historical and social context. Death and sex were phenomena very differently regarded in the Roman world to how we see them today in the supposedly enlightened and liberal 21st century. Both are still taboo subjects with a capacity still to shock and embarrass, requiring hushed tones in their discussion: in ancient Rome they required nothing of the sort.

Warfare and conflict were an inextricable and constant part of Roman life, from the foundation of the state in 753 BC to the eventual fall of the Roman Empire some 1,200 years later. And so were the innumerable deaths which always went with the wars and battles. The belligerence of the state was always integral to Roman political life: Roman bellicosity shaped their economy and defined their society. Josephus, writing in the 1st century AD, stated that the Roman people emerged from the womb carrying weapons. Centuries later, F. E. Adcock echoed these words when he said "a Roman was half a soldier from the start, and he would endure a discipline which soon produced the other half".

Rome's obsession with war stretched over her 1,200 years of history and saw Roman armies fighting in and garrisoning the full extent of her territories, from Parthia in the east (modern-day Iran) to Africa (Tunisia) and Aegyptus in the south (Egypt) and to Britannia in the cold northwest. There were few years in which there was no conflict: each summer, when the campaigning season began, an army was levied, consuls

The Christian martyrs' last prayer by Jean-Léon Gérôme (1824–1904). Gérôme identified the setting as ancient Rome's racecourse, the Circus Maximus. He noted such details as the goalposts and the chariot tracks in the dirt. The seating, however, more closely resembles that of the Colosseum, Rome's amphitheatre, in which gladiatorial combats and other spectacles were held. Similarly, the hill in the background surmounted by a colossal statue and a temple is nearer in appearance to the Athenian Acropolis than it is to Rome's Palatine Hill. The artist also commented on the religious fortitude of the victims who are about to suffer martyrdom either by being devoured by the wild beasts or by being smeared with pitch and set ablaze, which also never took place in the Circus Maximus. In this instance, Gérôme, whose paintings were usually admired for their sense of reality, has subordinated historical accuracy to drama.

or dictators took command, and battles were fought, before the army was disbanded at the close of the fighting year. Each summer, news would filter back to Roman and Italian families that husband, father, brother or cousin was not coming home. Death then through war was an accepted part of family life.

Death too was an accepted factor in childbirth: neonatal and maternal deaths were frequent and numerous: infant mortality may have been as high as thirty deaths in every one hundred pregnancies, compared with 9.1 per 1,000 in western Caucasian populations today. Thirty percent of all babies died before age one and fifty percent by age ten; these survivors would then have a fifty percent chance of reaching age fifty. Seventeen percent would see seventy.

Death was a good day out at the arena where gladiators, slaves, criminals, prisoners of war, religious non-conformists, and the disabled provided a regular diet of death for the baying masses, hungry for fights to the death or for end-of-life mutilation by wild animals. Suicide was a not uncommon way out of a difficult political situation, either voluntary or through coercion. Slaves were often abused and worked to death as a matter of course. To the average Roman then, the barbaric actions, the purges, assassinations and the massacres committed by their emperors might not have seemed quite as shocking as they are to us today.

The same is true of sex. The Romans had few of the hang-ups we have. Our 21st-century perspective on sex and sexuality is informed by the accumulation of years of baggage loaded onto us by centuries of change: the vacillating strictures of the church, the prudish Victorians and the permissive 1960s to name but three significant changing influences. Rome was somewhat different. The ubiquity of erotica in murals and mosaics, in sex manuals, poetry and plays, in phalluses, on coins and in ceramics, on walls as graffiti and even on tombstones would suggest that Romans were somewhat more relaxed and less exercised by the ways of the flesh, accustomed as they were to enjoying having sex around them, enjoying looking at sex. The shame, embarrassment and secrecy which accompanies erotica or pornography—itself a 19th-century term—in many societies today would have been quite alien to them: to the Roman, most sex was probably quite normal, an everyday part of everyday life. Importantly, the public display of erotica would of course have been seen by women as well as men, and by their children; the love poetry, the plays and the satires were read, heard and watched by literate women as well as literate men. Visual representations of sex in public and in the home, many of them featuring attractive partners of either sex (or both), reflected positive and healthy social attitudes enjoyed by homeowners and their guests alike. While much of the deviant and repellent behaviour of some of the emperors and empresses remains repellent and deviant, it was probably never quite as shocking to them as it is to some of us.

1. MONSTROUS BEHAVIOUR BEFORE ROME

Atrocious behaviour has been with us since the dawn of civilization. To give a couple of examples from the countless millions that no doubt took place before the founding of Rome in 753 BC, women were being physically and sexually assaulted by men as soon as man took to fighting fellow man: relatively recently, a 2,000-year-old adult female skeleton excavated in South Africa reveals that the woman was shot in the back with two arrows; a late Ice Age discovery from Sicily has unearthed a woman with an arrow in her pelvis.

Sargon of Akkad, probably our first great conqueror and the first ruler of the Semitic-speaking Akkadian Empire, is famous for his conquests of the Sumerian city-states between 2400 and 2300 BC. Among his conquests was Kazalla which he razed to the ground so comprehensively that the "birds could not find a place to perch away from the ground". He celebrated the conquest of Uruk and the victory over its leader Lugalzagesi, by leading him "in a collar to the gate of Enlil" in humiliation.

An equally disturbing instance of barbaric cruelty comes when we learn that the Israelites may have pioneered ethnic cleansing: they theologized (blamed their god for) their uncompromising reprisals when Yahweh was said to have decreed that the raiding Amalekites would be expunged from memory for all time—an early *damnatio memoriae* (lit. a damnation of memory)—for their attacks on and appropriation of Israelite settlements. This curse endured into the time of Samuel and Saul (c. 1100 BC) when the former ordered the latter to exterminate the Amalekites down to the last woman and child, and to erase their agrarian economy. Yahweh's sanction of the Amalekite genocide was indicative of the worrying fact that a warring state's actions, however execrable, could be justified and mitigated by the apparent will of God. Divine approval has been necessary before the opening of and during hostilities in many theatres of war throughout the ages; omens in the ancient world were there to be interpreted and had to be favourable before battle, while failure to observe them could be very costly. An imprudent and impious Naram-Sin lost 250,000 men when he chose to ignore ill omens before a battle. Divine sanction has often been a convenient tool in the convenient and conscience-salving justification and mitigation of unspeakable atrocities.

The Assyrians had a shocking reputation for mutilation, ripping open the stomachs of pregnant enemy women, as did some Egyptians, not least Amenophis II (or Amenhotep, 1439–1413 BC) who massacred all surviving opposition at Ugarit.

Above: Joshua fighting
Amalek in Exodus 17.
(Phillip Medhurst Collection)

Right: Sphinx head of a young
Amenhotep II. (Musée du
Louvre/ Iry-Hor)

The Egyptians were also infamous for systematically mutilating the defeated; for example, the detritus from the battle of Megiddo yielded eighty-three severed hands. The walls of the temple at Medinet Habu show piles of phalluses and hands which were hacked from Libyan invaders and their allies by Ramesses III (1193–1162 BC). Ashurbanipal, the Assyrian king who reigned from 668–627 BC, rejoiced in his violence, boasting, "I will hack up the flesh [of the defeated] and then carry it with me, to show off in other lands." His ostentatious brutality is widely depicted: one picture shows him implanting a dog chain through the cheek and jaw of a vanquished Bedouin king, Yatha, and then reducing him to a life in a dog kennel, where he guards the gate of Ninevah or hauls the royal chariot. Babylon was a particular threat; when Ashurbanipal destroyed the city he tore out the Babylonians' tongues before smashing them to death with their shattered statuary, and then fed their corpses—thoughtfully diced into little pieces—to the dogs, pigs, zibu birds, vultures, and fish. Ashur-etil-ilani (627–623 BC), Ashurbanipal's heir, had a predilection for cutting open the bellies of his opponents "as though they were young rams".

In the Bible we read of the children of the defeated being dashed to death, and, yet again, pregnant women having their stomachs ripped open. War rape was a constant; again in the Bible, the prophet Zechariah exults in the sexual violation of women; Isaiah's vision was equally apocalyptic when he states: "Their little children will be dashed to death before their eyes. Their homes will be sacked, and their wives will be raped." In Lamentations it is written that "women have been violated in Zion, and virgins in the towns of Judah".

Jezebel (d. 850 BC) was trouble for the Israelites. A Phoenician and probably the great aunt of Dido, queen of Carthage, she married King Ahab of Israel and brought with her a zeal for her religion, centred on Baal and Asherah, equal to the Israelites' devotion to Yahweh. Conflict was inevitable: Jezebel imposed her religion on Ahab and ruthlessly executed hundreds of prophets of Israel, forcing more into exile. Jezebel, however, was first up against Elijah, then Elisha and Jehu who eventually saw to it that she, dressed in all her finery and seductively made up, was thrown out of her window and consumed by ravenous dogs below. Her skull, her feet, and the palms of her hands were all that remained; Jehu's horse trampled on the corpse.

Nebuchadnezzar II (c. 630-562 BC) ruled Babylon from 605 BC until his death in 562 BC. He was the archetypal warrior king, "the destroyer of nations" and would tolerate "no opponent from horizon to sky".

A revolt in Judah in 588 BC led by Zedekiah provoked a merciless siege of Jerusalem which culminated in the city, including the First Temple, being totally razed and the inhabitants butchered. Zedekiah was forced to endure watching his sons being slaughtered before his own eyes were gouged out. The Jews were then deported east

Nebuchadnezzar by William Blake (1757–1827) (Tate Gallery, London)

where they mourned Zion "by the rivers of Babylon". Nebuchadnezzar's prowess on the battlefield was matched by a civic building programme second to none which saw armies of slave labour extend an extravagant royal palace including a public museum, possibly the world's first; he built a bridge over the Euphrates, constructed the Processional Way and the magnificent Ishtar Gate lavishly decorated with glazed brick, plus the wondrous Hanging Gardens of Babylon, a gift for his wife. The formidable city walls were fifty-six miles long and wide enough at the top to accommodate chariot races. Women enjoyed something like equal rights, education was promoted with schools and temples, other religions were tolerated and the arts flourished making Babylon a centre of culture in the region. Despite his ruthlessness and cruelty on the battlefield, he was a social reformer who defended the poor, criminalized bribery and corruption and strengthened the rule of law.

For the ancient Greeks too, rape came with the sanction of the gods. The Greek gods and heroes were rape role models: Zeus raped Leda in the form of a swan, Europa in the guise of a bull. He raped Danae disguised as a shower of rain. He raped Alkmen masquerading as her own husband. Zeus male-raped Ganymede. Antiope was raped

Nebuchadnezzar ordering the construction of the Hanging Gardens of Babylon to please his consort by Amyitis René-Antoine Houasse (1645–1710) (Palace of Versailles Salon de Vénus/ RMN)

by Zeus, Cassandra was raped by Ajax the Lesser, Chrysippus was raped by his tutor Laius, Persphone was raped by Hades, Medusa was raped by Poseidon, Philomela was raped by her brother-in-law, and the daughters of Leucippus, Phoebe and Hilaeira, were abducted, raped and later married to Castor and Pollux.

In the real world, the battle of Sepeia in 494 BC finally clinched for Sparta their dominance over the Argives in the struggle for supremacy in the Peloponnese. Based on information revealed to him by the oracle at Delphi, Cleomenes I of Sparta was inspired to lead an army to take Argos at Sepeia near Tiryns. A different oracle had warned the Argives of impending doom and to beware Spartan duplicity. So, in obedience to this, they instructed their herald to listen to what the Spartan herald said and repeat it verbatim to his Argive troops. Cleomenes soon caught on and told his men to charge and attack when given the order to take breakfast. The Argives were massacred as they ate and when the thousand or so survivors took refuge in a sacred grove nearby, Cleomenes simply set fire to it, ruthlessly killing all within.

After the siege of Olynthus in 479 BC the Persian forces massacred most of the inhabitants. In 431 BC the massacre of Plataea saw 150 Theban prisoners of war executed: Thucydides tells us that an armed force of 300 Thebans commanded by two leading Theban generals were admitted into Plataea by two private citizens who expected the Theban force to immediately capture and kill the democratic leaders and bring Plataea into alliance with Thebes. Instead the Plataeans killed over half of the 300 Thebans. Some of the remaining Thebans escaped with the help of a Plataean woman who provided them with an axe to break open one of the town gates. Some of the invaders tried to escape by jumping off the city wall, but most of these were killed in the fall. Others entered a large open building, mistaking it for an exit from the town. The Plataeans locked the building and held them there for a short time before killing them all. Four years later at the fall of Plataea in 427 BC two hundred Plataean and Athenian PoWs were executed.

Thucydides describes how the Thracians sacked Mycalessus and the women and children were put to the sword; but were the women raped beforehand? How often was rape committed during the euphemistic enslavement of women? The pupils in a boys' school there were certainly massacred. After the Mytilenean revolt in 427 BC a thousand ringleaders were executed without trial by the Athenians. The Helot massacre in 425 BC saw Sparta's brutal Krypteia (secret police) execute 2,000 Helot slaves. The Spartan suppression of the Helots was endless; this is what Myron of Priene of the middle 3rd century BC has to say: "They assign to the Helots every shameful task leading to disgrace. For they ordained that each one of them must wear a dog-skin cap [κυνῆ / kunê] and wrap himself in skins [διφθέρα/ diphthéra] and receive a stipulated number of beatings every year regardless of any wrongdoing, so that they would never forget they were slaves. Moreover, if any exceeded the vigour proper to a slave's condition, they made death the penalty; and they allotted a punishment to those controlling them if they failed."*

Plutarch describes the ritual humiliation they had to endure, that Spartans treated the Helots "harshly and cruelly ...also they compelled them to drink pure wine [which was considered dangerous, wine usually being diluted with water] ... and to lead them in that condition into their public halls, that the children might see what a sight a drunken man is; they forced them to dance low dances, and sing ridiculous songs ... during *syssitia* [obligatory banquets].†

In 423 BC, Scione revolted from Athens with support from the Spartans, resulting in the siege of the town which lasted for two years until 421 BC, even though the two enemies had earlier agreed a temporary peace treaty. Ultimately, the defenders of the city were either executed or sold into slavery. At the massacre of Hysiae in 417 BC all male citizens were murdered by the Spartans; the destruction of Melos the following year 416 BC saw all Melian men killed by the Athenians, their women and children enslaved.

In 335 BC Alexander the Great slew 6,000 men, women and children when he took the city of Thebes; 30,000 more were sold into slavery. In 315 BC Apollonides, governor of Argos, invaded Arcadia, and captured the town of Stymphalus. Back home the Argives promised to surrender their town to Alexander, the son of Polyperchon. Apollonides got wind of the plan and suddenly returned to Argos.

* Thucydides 7, 29.
† *Life of Lycurgus* 28, 8-10.

In this 14th-century Byzantine illustration Alexander the Great's infantry invades Athens. The horses of Alexander and his adjutant are represented as *cataphract* (armored cavalry). (*Alexander Romance* in S. Giorgio dei Greci, Venice)

About 500 senators were assembled in the prytaneum: Apollonides had all the doors of the house well guarded, so that none of them might escape, and then set fire to it. All perished. The other Argives who had taken part in the conspiracy were either exiled or put to death. In 213 at Messene 200 magistrates and their supporters were killed by demagogues supported by Macedon. In 167 BC, 550 Aetolian leaders were slain by Roman soldiers.

2. MONSTROUS BEHAVIOUR IN THE REPUBLIC

And so on into Rome where the foundation of the city reeks of rapine: in legend, the Sabine women were abducted as baby-makers and raped to guarantee the survival of the nascent Roman state; that paragon of Roman wifely chastity, Lucretia (d. c. 510 BC), was cruelly raped and took her life in shame, thus ensuring the foundation of the city. Verginia (c. 465 BC–449) was slain by her own solicitous father to avoid the very real prospect of being raped. Her death guaranteed the restoration of the Roman republic.

Carales and Beneventum (214 BC)

The Romans won a decisive victory at Carales, in Sardinia, under Titus Manlius Torquatus. The slaughter was extensive: 12,000 Sardinians and Carthaginians were killed, and Hasdrubal the Bald, Hanno, and Mago were all taken prisoner, along with 3,700 others. Hamsocora, the local chief who instigated the conflict, committed suicide when he learned that his son had been killed in the battle.

The following year Tiberius Sempronius Gracchus faced Hanno at Beneventum (Benevento). Gracchus's army consisted largely of the slaves who had joined up after Cannae. In an attempt to still their restlessness, and satisfy their yearning for their promised freedom, Gracchus declared that immediate liberty would be granted to every man who brought him a Carthaginian head. Mass decapitation followed; so intent were the slaves to deliver a head that they neglected to deal with the still-rampant living enemy, and were encumbered by the heads they were carrying under their arms. Gracchus had to back-pedal: he ordered the slaves to leave the corpses intact, and promised freedom to all—but only if the battle was won. The Carthaginians were slaughtered, with the massacre pursuing them all the way back to their camp. They lost 16,000 men to the Romans' two thousand. Gracchus kept his promise and freed the victorious slaves. Some 4,000 others, with whom he was less than pleased, were less fortunate: he ordered that they should eat their evening meal standing up, instead of sitting down, for the rest of their service in the legions. This same year, Marcus Claudius Marcellus stormed Leontini and put 2,000 Roman deserters—who were hiding in the city—to the sword.

Sieges generally seem to have brought out some of the worst atrocities perpetrated by the Romans, particularly the aftermath of sieges. They also generated exceptions to the general *iures belli* and rules of fair play; retribution and exacting reparations for the time, trouble, and lives expended by the Romans seem to have provided good enough reasons to reject the rule book. Frontinus tells how Sulla broke the siege at Preaeneste (in 82 BC): by sticking the heads of the enemy generals on spears, displaying them to the remaining inhabitants to break their resolve. Domitius Corbulo was especially brutal while besieging Tigranocerta in AD 60; he executed the noble Vadandus, whom he had captured, and shot his head out of a balista into the enemy camp. The human projectile landed in the middle of an enemy meeting, causing them to seek terms for surrender. Scenes 24, 72 and 57 of Trajan's Column depict Dacian heads on poles, and scene 147 shows the severed head of Decebalus, king of the Dacians. Of course, such atrocities were not exclusive to the Romans—Frontinus also tells us how in AD 9 the Germans, under Arminiuson, fastened the heads of dead Romans on spears and brought them to the Roman camp. The Germans did the same at Teutoburg Wald.

It seems that cities which surrendered, rather than being taken by storm, received a relative degree of clemency. Livy describes two such cases: Pometia in 502 BC and Phocaea in 190 BC. At Cartagena in 209 BC, Scipio stopped the wholesale slaughter (which included slicing dogs and other animals in half) once Mago had surrendered. The clear message from the Romans was that resistance was not worth the vicious reprisals that would inevitably follow; in that respect, holding out in a siege was no different from any other form of anti-Roman hostility. In 216 BC Capua induced retribution when the inhabitants locked a number of Roman citizens in a steaming, airless bath-house, where they died a terrible death. At Uxellodunum

The reliefs of Trajan's Column by Conrad Cichorius. (Graphics 1896)

in 51 BC, Julius Caesar had the enemies' hands cut off as a terrible and visible warning to anyone else contemplating resistance.

The Lusitanians had defeated Servius Sulpicius Galba in 151 BC at the battle of Cauca. The same year, L. Licinius Lucullus, notorious for his brutality, arrived in Spain as consul. With no provocation and without senatorial authority he attacked the Vaccaei even though they had no quarrel with Rome. On a spurious excuse for war, Lucullus attacked Cauca and slew 3,000 of the Vaccaei; the following day they requested peace and compliantly agreed to all of the Romans' terms. This did not, however, stop Lucullus entering the town and butchering the surviving adult males.

In 150 BC Lucullus joined up with Galba and attacked with such ferocity that the Lusitanians surrendered. In the subsequent negotiations, however, Galba showed himself to be just as duplicitous as Lucullus. The Lusitanians were persuaded to leave their homes on the promise of a life in better lands in other regions. However, a trench was dug around them to prevent their escape and they were massacred. The only thing this atrocious act of ethnic cleansing actually achieved was a stronger resolve among the Lusitanians to resist the Romans. Their time was to come in 147 BC when Viriathus, a natural guerrilla fighter, burst onto the scene.

Mithridates

In 90 BC, Mithridates, king of Pontus and Armenia Minor in northern Anatolia, expelled Nicomedes from Bithynia and Ariobarzanes from Cappadocia. The Roman general Manlius lost 10,000 soldiers at Protopachium where, incidentally, more prisoners were taken, treated decently and released; Manlius fled to Pergamum. Mithridates had won and was free to move around the region without impediment. For Rome it was disaster; but worse was to follow: it was at this time that Mithridates ordered the extermination of all Romans and Italians in the Asiatic Vespers. In 88 BC Mithridates received some sinister and mischievous advice from a leading Greek philosopher at his court, Metrodoros of Skepsis, *ho misoromaios*, the Roman-hater. Metrodoros convinced the king that if he wanted to bring more communities on side against the Romans he should exterminate all Romans in the province regardless of age or sex; this was the only way to be rid of Roman rule forever. The massacre was clinically executed and timed to take the victims by surprise, in every community and simultaneously. In a letter to all the civic authorities Mithridates stipulated that the atrocity was to happen one month after the date of his letter.

Appian takes up the gruesome story, its precision and insidious planning: "[Mithridates] wrote secretly to all his satraps and magistrates that on the thirtieth day thereafter they should set upon all Romans and Italians in their towns, and upon their wives and children and their domestics of Italian birth, kill them and throw their bodies out unburied, and share their goods with himself. He threatened to punish any who should bury the dead or conceal the living, and offered rewards to informers and to those who should kill persons in hiding, and freedom to slaves for betraying their masters. To debtors for killing money-lenders he offered release from one half of their obligations."

Appian continues: "The Ephesians tore fugitives, who had taken refuge in the temple of Artemis, from the very images of the goddess and slew them. The Pergameans shot with arrows those who had fled to the temple of Aesculapius, while they were still clinging to his statues. The Adramytteans followed those who sought to escape by swimming, into the sea, and killed them and drowned their children. The Caunii, who had been made subject to Rhodes after the war against [the Seleucid king Antiochus III] and had been lately liberated by the Romans, pursued the Italians who had taken refuge about the Vesta statue of the senate house, tore them from the shrine, killed children before their mothers' eyes, and then killed the mothers themselves and their husbands after them. The citizens of Tralles, in order to avoid the appearance of blood-guiltiness, hired a savage monster named Theophilus, of Paphlagonia, to do the work. He conducted the victims to the temple of Concord, and there murdered them, chopping off the hands of some who were embracing the sacred images."

Glorying in his success, Mithridates now eyed Europe. His crony Aristion stirred up unrest in Athens and was made tyrant there; the city Piraeus and other parts of southern and central Greece were taken. The Roman Sulla then came in pursuit and won over most of the Greek states. Athens, nevertheless, remained loyal to Mithridates, and was subjected to a brutal, merciless siege through the winter of 87 and 86. Athens fell to Sulla on 1 March 86 BC when the water ran out and the Athenians were dying of starvation; the city and its citizens were severely punished as a warning to others contemplating such insolent and anti-Roman behaviour. Appian: "Knowing that the defenders of Athens were severely pressed by hunger, that they had devoured all their cattle, boiled the hides and skins, and licked what they could get from them, and that some had even eaten human flesh, Sulla directed his soldiers to encircle the city with a ditch so that the inhabitants might not escape secretly, even one by one. This done, he brought up his ladders and at the same time began to break through the wall. The feeble defenders were soon put to flight, and the Romans rushed into the city.'"*

Sulla

A great and pitiless slaughter ensued in Athens, the inhabitants, for want of nourishment, being too weak to escape. Sulla ordered an indiscriminate massacre, sparing

---

*   Appian, *Mithridatic Wars.*

neither women nor children. He was angry that they had so suddenly joined the barbarians without cause, and had displayed such violent animosity toward him. Most of the Athenians, when they heard the order given, rushed upon the swords of the slayers voluntarily. Sulla forbade the burning of the city, but allowed the soldiers to plunder it. In many houses they found human flesh prepared for food. The next day Sulla sold the slaves at auction.

Things came to a head on 1 November 82 BC when Sulla clashed with the Marian and Samnite armies at the decisive battle of the Colline Gate, on the outskirts of Rome. Plutarch tells how Sulla's entry was devastating in the extreme: "[Sulla] shouted orders to torch the houses and, seizing a blazing firebrand, led the

Sulla. (Glyptothek Munich/ José Luiz Bernardes Ribeiro)

way himself, ordering his archers to use their fire-bolts and shoot them up at the roofs. This was no calm or collected tactic, but done in passion; having surrendered the control over his actions to his anger ... he made his entry by fire, which did not discriminate between the guilty and the innocent."

Although Sulla suffered an unexpected heavy reverse on his left flank, he won the day in a narrow victory when the Samnites and the Marian army both collapsed: more than 50,000 troops died that day. Sulla systematically murdered what was left of the opposition and emerged as the undisputed master of Rome.

Three thousand Marian troops were captured while another 3,000 surrendered; all were imprisoned on the Campus Martius until executed. Their corpses were thrown into the Tiber which became clogged with bodies: an estimated 10,000 men perished in this way. Sulla had Marius's ashes exhumed and flung into the Tiber. He wasted no time in flexing his newfound political muscle, and he did so with prodigious savagery, inflicting on the Roman people a terrifying programme of proscriptions, the like of which was unprecedented, even by the standards of those set by Marius and Cinna a few years earlier. According to Plutarch, "Sulla now made the blood flow, filling the city with numberless and limitless deaths without number or limit," adding that many of the murdered had nothing to do with Sulla, but he butchered them anyway to "please his hangers on" and, if anyone thought they had escaped the massacre, then let them think again: for there was more to come: "Sulla straightaway proscribed eighty men with no recourse to any magistrate. This evoked a murmur [of disapproval] so he let one day pass, and then proscribed 220 more, with just as many on the third day. Haranguing the people about this he said that he had proscribed everyone he could think of but those who now escaped his memory, he would proscribe them at some time in the future."

Sulla's proscription policy was ostensibly payback for the atrocities perpetrated by Marius and Cinna and to liquidate anyone whom he considered to have acted against the best interests of the Republic while he was away fighting Mithridates. To that end he ordered the execution, over a number of months, of some 1,500 senators and equites, although some put the figure at nearer nine thousand. Many others were exiled.

The dictat was nothing if not rigorous and exhaustive: there was literally no hiding place: aiding or sheltering a proscribed person was a capital offence; on the other hand, murdering a proscribed person attracted a reward of two talents. The aim was simply to have as many people on the proscription lists brought in, dead or alive. Significantly, family members were included in the punishment, and slaves qualified for the rewards. This, of course, made it impossible for normal family life to go on while making it attractive for slaves to make some easy money. Consequently, as Plutarch tells us, "husbands were butchered in the arms of their wives, sons in the arms of their mothers."

It turns out that many of the proscribed had no connection with Sulla or with his faction and were certainly not his enemies; they were killed for their property, which was confiscated and auctioned off. Sulla made a tidy profit as the proceeds from these sales easily covered the cost of rewarding those who killed the proscribed. Sulla, with an eye on possible future retribution, banned the sons and grandsons of the proscribed banned from running for political office for the next thirty years.

Spartacus

The scattered remnants of Spartacus's army took refuge in the mountains of Bruttium where, led by one Publipor, they organized themselves into four groups on the banks of the river Silarus and conducted a guerrilla war against the Romans until they were finally wiped out by Pompey and Crassus.

The crucified slaves by Fedor Andreevich Bronnikov (1827–1902). (Tretyakov Gallery, Moscow)

The Romans captured 6,000 unfortunate slaves alive. As a stark, rotting reminder of the fate which awaits the rebellious slave, they were all crucified on crosses placed every forty metres or so along the 150 miles of the Via Appia between Rome and Capua; the corpses were gradually eaten away by wild dogs and carrion. Pompey butchered a further 5,000 'survivors'. By contrast, 3,000 Roman prisoners of war were found at Spartacus's camp at Rhegium, alive and well.

Fulvia Flacca Bambula

The ambitious and assertive Fulvia Flacca Bambula (c. 83–40 BC), is famous for gleefully pricking the decapitated Cicero's tongue with a hairpin: she took exception and revenge after Cicero had insinuated that Mark Antony, her third husband, only married her for her money. Cicero's head was on public display in the Forum after his proscription in 43 BC. Fulvia too is likened to a man—"a woman in body alone"—by Velleius Paterculus who evidently regarded her vengeful and gruesome act as unlady-like and by implication the sort of thing only a man should do.

This is Cassius Dio's account: "Fulvia took the head into her hands before it was removed, and after abusing it spitefully and spitting upon it, set it on her knees, opened the mouth, and pulled out the tongue, which she pierced with the pins that she used for her hair, at the same time uttering many brutal jests."

Fulvia with the head of Cicero by Pavel Svedomsky (1849–1904).

Pomponia, the widow of Cicero's brother, Quintus Tullius, and sister of Atticus was even more sadistic: when Philologus, the freedman who betrayed the Ciceros, was brought to her she ordered him to cut off strips of his own flesh, cook them and then eat them.

Salome

Salome (c. AD 14 –c. 62 and 71) was the daughter of Herod II and Herodias. She is famous for demanding and getting the head of John the Baptist. According to Mark's gospel, "a daughter of Herodias's danced before Herod and her mother Herodias on his birthday, and in doing so gave her mother the opportunity to obtain the head of John the Baptist". Herodias bore a grudge against John for stating that Herod's marriage to her was unlawful; she encouraged her daughter to demand that John be executed: "A convenient day arrived when Herod spread an evening meal on his birthday for his high officials and the military command-ers and the most prominent men of Galilee. The daughter of Herodias came in and danced, pleasing Herod and those dining with him. The king said to the girl: 'Ask me for whatever you want, and I will give it to you.' Yes, he swore to her: 'Whatever you ask me for, I will give it to you, up to half my kingdom.' So she went out and said to her mother: 'What should I ask for?' She said: 'The head of John the Baptiser.' She immediately rushed in to the king and made her request, saying: 'I want you to give me right away on a platter the head of John the Baptist.' Although this deeply grieved him, the king did not want to disregard her request, because of his oaths and his guests. So the king immediately sent a bodyguard and

Salome as portrayed
by Titian (1490–1576)
c. 1515. (Doria Pamphilj
Gallery, Rome)

commanded him to bring John's head. So he went off and beheaded him in the
prison and brought his head on a platter. He gave it to the girl, and the girl gave it
to her mother. When his disciples heard of it, they came and took his body and laid
it in a tomb." (Mark 6:21–29)

Herod the Great

Herod the Great (74–c. 4 BC), Roman client king of Judea, is another of history's
paradoxes. He suffered throughout his lifetime from depression and paranoia. On
the one hand there is his extensive and impressive programme of building projects
throughout Judea, including the Temple Mount in Jerusalem, the construction of the
port at Caesarea Maritima deploying cutting-edge technology in hydraulic cement
and underwater construction, the fortress at Masada, and Herodium. On the other
hand there is his despotic rule suppressing his people, particularly Jews, and their
opposition to him; oppressive taxation to pay for his building programme; his use

Massacre of the innocents by Matteo di Giovanni (1435–95) in 1488. (Museo Nazionale di Capodimonte)

of secret police to monitor and report the feelings of the general public towards him; banning protests, and removing opponents by force; his bodyguard of 2,000 soldiers.

And then there is the Massacre of the Innocents as described by Matthew and according to whom, following the birth of Jesus, magi from the East visited Herod to inquire the whereabouts of "the one having been born king of the Jews", because they had seen his star in the east wanted to pay him homage. Herod, who thought *he* was king of the Jews, was alarmed and convened the chief priests and scribes of the people and asked them where the 'Anointed One' (the Messiah, Greek:

Bethlehemitischer kindermord, or Herod's slaughter of all male infants in Bethlehem, a version by Rubens. (Stadtbibliothek, Trier)

Ὁ Χριστός, ho Christos) was to be born. They answered, in Bethlehem, citing Micah 5:2. Herod therefore sent the magi to Bethlehem, slyly instructing them to search for the child and, after they had found him, to "report to me, so that I too may go and worship him". However, after they had found Jesus, they were warned in a dream not to report back to Herod. Similarly, a dream told Joseph that Herod intended to kill Jesus, so he and his family fled to Egypt. When Herod learnt of this he issued a decree to kill all boys of the age of two and under in Bethlehem and its vicinity. Joseph and his family stayed in Egypt until Herod's death, then moved to Nazareth to avoid living under Herod's son Archelaus.

The first non-Christian reference to the massacre is recorded four centuries later by Macrobius (c. AD 395–423), who writes in his *Saturnalia*: "When he [emperor Augustus] heard that among the boys in Syria under two years old whom Herod, king of the Jews, had ordered killed, his own son was also killed, he said: it is better to be Herod's pig, than his son."

The historicity of the massacre is problematic. Herod committed many atrocities, not least, as reported by Josephus, murdering three of his own sons, his mother-in-law and his second wife but, Matthew apart, no other contemporary sources refer to the massacre. One explanation for the absence of corroboration might be that Bethlehem was a small village, and thus the number of male children under the age of two may have been as few as twenty—nothing that remarkable in those days.

Herod died in Jericho following an eye-wateringly painful, putrefying mysterious illness known to posterity as 'Herod's Evil'. Josephus describes it in lurid detail: "But now Herod's distemper greatly increased upon him after a severe manner, and this by God's judgment upon him for his sins; for a fire glowed in him slowly, which did not so much appear to the touch outwardly, as it augmented his pains inwardly; for it brought upon him a vehement appetite to eating, which he could not avoid to supply with one sort of food or other. His entrails were also ex-ulcerated, and the chief violence of his pain lay on his colon; an aqueous and transparent liquor also had settled itself about his feet, and a like matter afflicted him at the bottom of his belly. Nay, further, his privy-member was putrefied, and produced worms; and when he sat upright, he had a difficulty of breathing, which was very loathsome, on account of the stench of his breath, and the quickness of its returns; he had also convulsions in all parts of his body, which increased his strength to an insufferable degree. It was said by those who pretended to divine, and who were endued with wisdom to foretell such things, that God inflicted this punishment on the king on account of his great impiety; yet was he still in hopes of recovering, though his afflictions seemed greater than any one could bear."[*]

Josephus also says that the pain of his illness led Herod to attempt suicide by stabbing, and that the attempt was thwarted by his cousin. In some much later narratives and depictions, the attempt succeeds; for example, in the 12th-century Eadwine Psalter.

---

[*] It was possibly arteriosclerosis, which, when accompanied by deterioration of the heart and kidneys, would result in the symptoms described.

3. THE IMPERIAL MONSTERS

Tiberius (42 BC–AD 37)

"While his mother lived, he was a mixture of good and evil; he was infamous for his cruelty, though he veiled his debaucheries, while he loved or feared Sejanus. Finally, he plunged into every wickedness and disgrace, when fear and shame being cast off, he simply indulged his own inclinations."

Tacitus, *Annals* 6, 50-51

Tiberius Caesar by Aegidius Sadeler II (1570–1629).

Tiberius was Roman emperor from AD 14 to AD 37; he was Rome's second emperor, succeeding Augustus. Tiberius was the son of Tiberius Claudius Nero and Livia Drusilla, later Augustus's wife, and took the name Tiberius Claudius Nero. When his mother divorced Nero and married Octavian—later Augustus– Tiberius officially became Augustus's stepson. Tiberius later married Augustus's daughter from his marriage to Scribonia, the wayward Julia the Elder, and was later adopted by Augustus, making him a member of the Julian *gens* and assuming the name Tiberius Julius Caesar as a member of the Julio-Claudian dynasty. Tiberius was the grand-uncle of Caligula, paternal uncle of Claudius, and great-grand-uncle of Nero.

Tiberius's relationships with the women in his life obviously left their mark. With Livia, his bullying, meddling mother, and a wife whom he loved but was compelled to divorce for a third wife he resented, all of this obviously left Tiberius with issues that jaundiced his relationships with his women. Things started to go wrong when Julia began to assert her own individuality, reacting, no doubt to a greater or lesser extent, to the oppressed childhood she had endured, the increasingly liberal society around her and the sexual hypocrisy of her father as clearly manifested in his private life which was at odds with his legislation. When she was a girl there were reports, *vulgo existimabatur*, in the general opinion, of Julia's serial adultery with Sempronius Gracchus, described by Tacitus as *pervicax adulter*, a persistent adulterer, and rumours of an unhealthy relationship with her stepbrother, Tiberius. Suetonius describes Julia's behaviour as "all kinds of vice". In 12 BC Agrippa, her husband, died suddenly in Campania after an inconclusive winter campaign. Anxious about the succession, Augustus moved quickly and, as soon as Julia, still in mourning, had given birth to Agrippa Postumus, betrothed Julia to Tiberius, his stepson.

But Tiberius was already happily married, so with huge reluctance he was forced to divorce Vipsania Agrippina who was pregnant with their second child. Vipsania had been betrothed to Tiberius at birth when Tiberius was ten years old; they married in 19 BC. The divorce took place in 11 BC, "not without considerable pain" on Tiberius's part, and was a constant source of anguish to him for the rest of his life. One day Tiberius saw Vipsania in the street and became so distraught that official measures were taken to prevent a recurrence of the painful sighting.

Suetonius records that, despite a happy start to the new marriage, "living in harmony and with mutual affection" (*primo concorditer et amore mutuo vixit*), Tiberius soon came to loathe Julia. The feeling was mutual. Two events early on in their marriage had a significant impact. These could have brought the couple closer together, but, as it happened, they had the opposite effect. Firstly, their son died in infancy at Aquileia; secondly, in 9 BC, Drusus (Tiberius's devoted brother) was killed in a riding accident in Germany. Tiberius now condemned Julia's behaviour, her *mores*, possibly feeling guilty

Statue of Tiberius of Priverno, made shortly after AD 37.
(Museo Chiaramonti of the Vatican Museums)

Julia Augustus. (Altes Museum/ Miguel Hermoso Cuesta)

over their alleged incest of earlier years. Meanwhile, she considered him beneath her (*ut imparem*); she sent Augustus a letter, delivered by her lover, Sempronius Gracchus, which spelt this out. Tacitus says that Gracchus persistently undermined Julia's relationship with Tiberius, and even composed the damning letter. Suetonius, in his *Life of Tiberius*, reports that they were now sleeping in separate beds. By 6 BC, Tiberius had had enough; when he took refuge in Rhodes as a private citizen, having renounced all of his duties, the couple was separated by more than their beds.

Livia, Augustus's wife and empress of Rome, had pushed relentlessly for Tiberius to succeed Augustus, and when she succeeded she continually meddled in affairs of state where she, by Roman convention, had no business meddling. This irked Tiberius no end, a man who, despite his proven expertise as a military commander, had little or no interest in politics or empires, or even in ruling empires. 'Saturnine' is one word which defines him, a mood brought on by his mother's constant interference and by that forced termination of a very happy marriage.

'Depraved' is another defining epithet: we know about the allegations of impropriety with Julia, cross-dressing, group sex, his prodigious library of sex manuals and his notorious pederasty. According to Suetonius and Tacitus, there was more, much more.

Unable to tolerate an increasingly suffocating Rome and his mother's controlling influence any longer, Tiberius deserted the capital in AD 26 and took himself to Capri in self-imposed exile, leaving the satanic Sejanus to run the empire more or less as he pleased. Tiberius had found the splendid isolation he had long craved, but he was never isolated, except perhaps in a geographic sense. Suetonius tells of the sex club he had specially built in the Villa Jovis as a seedy venue for his clandestine depravity and how he had trawled his empire, dredging up girls and young men expert in unnatural copulation (*monstrosi concubitus*). He called them his *spintriae*, turning him on with their troilism. Aulus Vitellius, one of the short lived emperors of AD 79, is rumoured to have been one of these *spintriae*. He was seduced on Capri by Tiberius while an adolescent: his virginity was cheaply lost in order to help his father along his *cursus honorum*, in his running for office.

The most obscene paintings and statues were all around in ante-rooms, with a ready reference—a famous book on sexual positions, a Roman *Kama Sutra*, written by the famous sex writer Elephantis of Egypt—on hand for consultation. Suetonius tells that Tiberius packed a copy when he left for his retreat on Capri; Martial says it is "[a book] with intriguing new ways of making love". Suetonius tells us that Tiberius was an inveterate collector of sex manuals and owned a prodigious collection of erotic art; his pièce de résistance was a painting of Atalanta giving fellatio to Meleager, a work valued by the emperor at more than a million sesterces.

Outside in the woods he had boys and girls role-playing, dressed up as Pans and nymphs pleasuring each other in the caves. In the sea, Tiberius played a particularly odious game in which trained little boys, his *pisciculi*, 'minnows', chased him and got between his legs to lick and nibble at him. Even breastfeeding babies were not safe from his deviant behaviour; he made them suck away at his breast and in his groin. Once, while performing a sacrifice, he took a fancy to the boy carrying the incense and his brother trumpeter: both were sodomized and when they protested he broke their legs. Tiberius's cruel misogyny knew no bounds; one unfortunate victim was a woman called Mallonia, whom he seduced. When she showed him just how repellent she found him he had her followed by informers and, inevitably, she ended up in court. He railed at her, demanding an apology; she went home and committed suicide, but not before delivering another invective against the "foul-mouthed, hairy, stinking old man"—or, put another way, "the old goat goes for the mother goat with his tongue".

Tacitus corroborates Suetonius's account. He describes the emperor's sojourn on Capri as being spent shamed by the evil deeds and depravities into which he had hurled himself. He had corrupted and destroyed the innocence of the children of free-born citizens; so unnatural was his depravity that some of his activities had no Latin words to describe them and had to be coined. He even used slaves as predators and for stalking and procuring victims, rewarding the complicit and threatening those who resisted; violence and force was shown to uncooperative parents, Tiberius was happy to treat them as you would a prisoner of war— presumably with rape and murder.

A simple story related by Suetonius illustrates well just how nasty a person Tiberius was. One day, in an act of simple kindness and pride, a local fisherman presented a large mullet he had caught to the emperor: "A fisherman appeared unexpectedly and offered him a huge mullet; whereupon in his alarm that the man had clambered up to him from the back of the island over rough and pathless rocks, [Tiberius] had the poor fellow's face scrubbed with the fish." With commendable resignation the fisherman shrugs off the no doubt very painful exfoliation but, soon regrets it because "in the midst of his torture the man thanked his stars that he had not given the Emperor an enormous crab that he had caught, [however] Tiberius had his face ripped with the crab as well."

While Tiberius was indulging in his perversity on Capri, he had left the government of Rome in the treacherous hands of Lucius Aelius Sejanus, a hitherto loyal servant of the imperial family but now in command of the 12,000-strong Praetorian Guard. The temptations offered by this power culminated with Sejanus attempting to insinuate himself in and ingratiate himself with the Julian family line with a view to achieving the emperorship. His subsequent plot involved the overthrow of Tiberius. In AD 31 Sejanus was tried and executed; Tiberius enthusiastically followed this up with a campaign of terror on the largely Julian conspirators, as graphically described by Tacitus: "Executions were now a stimulus to his fury, and he ordered the death of all who were lying in prison under accusation of complicity with Sejanus. There lay, singly or in heaps, the unnumbered dead, of every age and sex, the illustrious with the obscure. Kinsfolk and friends were not allowed to be near them, to weep over them, or even to gaze on them too long. Spies were set round them, who noted the sorrow of each mourner and followed the rotting corpses, till they were dragged to the Tiber, where, floating or driven on the bank, no one dared to burn or to touch them."

LUCIUS AELIUS SEJANUS (20 BC–AD 31) was a friend of Tiberius. He was head of the Praetorian Guard from AD 14 until his death in AD 31. He developed the unit from an innocuous imperial bodyguard to a much-feared political force of 12,000 troops, which dispensed high-profile arbitrary justice and summary executions in the name of public order and security. To Tiberius, Sejanus was, in the report by Tacitus (*Annals* 4, 2) "my ally in my troubles". After years of increasing conflict with Drusus Julius Caesar, the son and potential heir of Tiberius, Sejanus seduced Livilla, Drusus's wife: the couple brought about the murder of Drusus by poisoning in AD 23. When Tiberius retreated to Capri in AD 26, seemingly oblivious of his friend's complicity, Sejanus effectively became de facto ruler of Rome, with designs on the lives of Agrippina's sons, Nero Caesar, Drusus Caesar, and Caligula, now potential successors to Tiberius.

Only Livia acted as a check on Sejanus, but this ended on her death in AD 29. Sejanus initiated a purge of senators and equestrians in Rome, removing any who might challenge his power. Networks of spies and informers brought the victims to trial on trumped-up charges of treason, with many choosing suicide over the disgrace of being condemned and executed. Agrippina and two of her sons, Nero and Drusus, were arrested and exiled in AD 30, and later starved to death in suspicious circumstances. Only Caligula, the last remaining son of Germanicus, survived the purges, by moving to Capri with Tiberius in AD 31.

Dio sums up the perilous situation in Rome: "Sejanus was so great a person by reason both of his excessive pride and of his vast power, that, to put it briefly, he himself seemed to be the emperor and Tiberius a kind of island potentate, inasmuch as the latter spent his time on the island of Capreae."

At the end of AD 31, Tiberius finally woke up to the situation; Sejanus was arrested, strangled and his body shoved down the Gemonian stairs where a mob tore his body to pieces. Riots followed, in which crowds hunted down and murdered anyone linked to Sejanus. A *damnatio memoriae* was issued by the Senate, and Sejanus's eldest son Strabo was arrested and executed. Upon learning of his death, Apicata, Sejanus's wife committed suicide but not before sending a letter to Tiberius, claiming that Drusus had been poisoned with the complicity of Livilla, accusations corroborated by confessions from Livilla's slaves, who, under torture, admitted to having administered the poison to Drusus.

Tiberius then went on a killing spree of his own. Livilla was starved to death by her mother Antonia Minor. The remaining children of Sejanus, Capito Aelianus and Junilla, were executed and because there was no precedent for the capital punishment of a virgin, Junilla was raped first, with the rope around her neck. Their bodies were thrown unceremoniously down the Gemonian stairs and Livilla was awarded her own *damnatio memoriae*.

Bilbilis mint L. Aelius Sejanus, praetorian consul, Struck AD 31, the name of Sejanus removed *in damnatio memoriae*. (SNG Copenhagen)

Caligula (AD 12–41)

"*Vivo!* I live on!"

Tacitus, reporting the dying words of Caligula

Caligula, or Gaius Julius Caesar Augustus Germanicus, was Roman emperor from AD 37 to AD 41. The son of Germanicus and Agrippina the Elder, he was the third of six surviving children. Gaius had two older brothers, Nero and Drusus, as well as three younger sisters, Agrippina the Younger, Julia Drusilla and Julia Livilla. He was also a nephew of Claudius, Germanicus's younger brother and his successor as emperor. He earned his sobriquet, Caligula, from the little army boots, (the diminutive form of *caliga*), he wore as a three-year-old trotting around the camps in which his father served in Germania.

Even by the standards of Tiberius's turbulent Rome Caligula's early life was fraught with life-changing trauma, insecurity and anxiety. The witch hunt carried out by Sejanus against his close family must have haunted the boy endlessly, as would aspects of the gloomy, hostile and dangerous forests of northern Germany where his father had to be bailed out by his mother when the general lost control of and respect from his mutinous legions. How far Caligula was shielded from all of this it is impossible to know but it is reasonable to assume that the tensions caused by the desperate military situation in Germania and its very un-Roman resolution by a woman percolated down to affect the young boy. After his father's death Agrippina returned to Rome with the children midst popular rejoicing, only to begin a relentless struggle with Tiberius which culminated in the execution of most of his family at the hands of Sejanus and his agents, a fate which Caligula, then aged nineteen, only escaped by joining Tiberius in his depravities on Capri.

Furthermore, both Seneca and Suetonius record that Caligula was physically repulsive; presumably they got this information, statues apart, from contemporary physiognomists who believed that outward appearance reflected inner character: the more repellent the look, the more monstrous the behaviour. Suetonius tells us that Caligula used to practise in front of a mirror to make himself more terrifying while Seneca asserts that to look at Caligula was in itself a form of torture.

Caligula was never an inconspicuous child or adolescent. From his early days dressed up as a soldier he graduated to impersonating Alexander the Great, a triumphant general or one of Rome's gods—precocious signs of delusions of grandeur. His normal attire was jazzed up with jewellery or ostentatious embroidery, precious stones and exotic sandals.

When Tiberius died in Misenum on 16 March AD 37, aged seventy-eight, Caligula was not very far away. In any event all our sources differ in their accounts of

Above: A Roman soldier's *caliga.*

Right: Caligula. (Pallazzo Massimo, Rome/Tomk2ski)

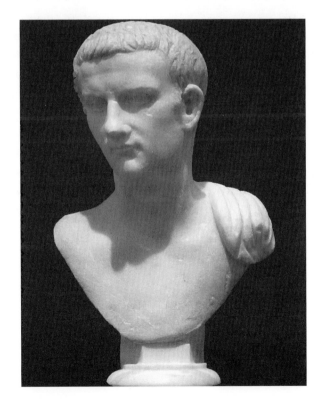

Caligula's alleged implication: Tacitus relates that Tiberius appeared to have stopped breathing but revived and was getting better; Macro, Prefect of the Praetorian Guard, smothered him anyway with his bedclothes. Suetonius says that the emperor was poisoned by Caligula, starved, and smothered with a pillow only to recover, and died while trying to get up from his couch. According to Dio, Caligula refused Tiberius food, insisting that it was warmth he needed, not food; then, assisted by Macro, he smothered the emperor in his bedclothes.

Whatever the facts, it may be reasonable to assume that Caligula had a hand in the death of his grand-uncle. However, Seneca the Elder and Philo, who both wrote during Tiberius's reign, as well as Josephus, record Tiberius as dying a natural death.

Such a traumatic and unsettling childhood cannot have failed to have impacted on Caligula psychologically and socially. One early manifestation of disturbance was his serial incest with his sisters. According to Suetonius, this was a regular, public occurrence, even in the presence of his wives. Indeed, his grandmother, Antonia Minor, once caught him in bed with Drusilla when they were staying at her house.

This unnatural behaviour soon developed into a cavalier and perverted attitude to women generally. Caligula seduced Ennia Naevia, the wife of Macro, the commander of the Praetorian Guard and an ally. He promised, in writing, that he would marry her when he became emperor. Other victims included Nymphidia, daughter of Callistus; the wife of Valerius Asiaticus; the concubine Pyrallis; Mnester the actor; Valerius Catullus and his brother-in-law, Marcus Lepidus.

Things started to get bad for Caligula and his mother in AD 29 when relations with Tiberius started rapidly deteriorating: Tiberius forbade Agrippina to

Caligula by Aegidius Sadeler II (1570–1629) c. 1600.

remarry, paranoid that any future husband would pose a threat to him. Agrippina and Caligula's brother, Nero, were banished on charges of treason.

Caligula was then sent to live with his great-grandmother, and Tiberius's domineering mother Livia. When Livia died that same year he was shipped off to live with his grandmother Antonia Minor. In AD 30, his brother Drusus Caesar was imprisoned on charges of treason while his other brother Nero died in exile from either starvation or suicide. Suetonius reports that after the banishment of his mother and brothers, life for the itinerant Caligula and his sisters was more or less as prisoners of Tiberius under close guard. In AD 33, both Caligula's mother and his brother Drusus died in captivity which left only Caligula and his three sisters.

Caligula married four women who had the misfortune to stray into his orbit: the first was Junia Claudilla (d. c. AD 34) also known as Junia Claudia; they were married

Caligula depositing the ashes of his mother and brother in the tomb of his ancestors by Eustache Le Sueur (1616–55) in 1647. (Royal Collection Windsor Castle)

at Antium in 33, but she died soon after giving birth to Caligula's first child, which also did not survive. In AD 37, heightened concerns about his succession may have prompted Caligula's marriage to Livia Orestilla (or Cornelia Orestina, according to Dio); they separated within the year on the grounds of her infertility. In his *Life of Caligula* Suetonius records that he actually appropriated Livia Orestilla during her wedding ceremony to Gaius Piso, carting her off to his palace after the quickest of divorces; Caligula issued a proclamation the next day that he had acquired a new wife in the tradition of Romulus and Augustus, who had both stolen wives from other men. She too did not last the year and two years after her peremptory dismissal was banished from Rome for allegedly going back to Piso; both Orestilla and Piso were banished for adultery to distant, solitary islands.

The rich and beautiful Lollia Paulina was his next victim; Caligula was attracted to her because someone happened to mention that Lollia's grandmother had been beautiful. Caligula made Lollia divorce her husband, Publius Memmius Regulus, to allow his marriage to her. Six months later he divorced her, because she too was supposedly barren; he then sentenced her to eternal celibacy, forbidding her to have sex with any other man, a sentence more commonly seen on a curse tablet.

Caligula then married Milonia Caesonia in AD 39; Suetonius says that she was neither beautiful nor young, but she was fertile, having had three children from a previous marriage. She was extravagant and louche, but Caligula seemingly loved her: she was Caligula's kind of woman and he never tired of showing her off before his troops, parading her dressed up in combat uniform and bearing a shield. He even made her parade, naked, before his friends. Caesonia gave birth to their daughter, Julia Drusilla, one month after their wedding—he refused to call Caesonia his wife until she had produced a child. Caligula never had any doubts that Julia Drusilla was his child, as her violent temper and habit of trying to scratch out the eyes of her friends left him in no doubt regarding his paternity.

In AD 35, Caligula was named joint heir to Tiberius's estate along with Tiberius Gemellus, son of Drusus and Livilla, the grandson of Tiberius and Caligula's second cousin.

After Tiberius's death, Caligula entered Rome on 28 March AD 37 as emperor; a joyous crowd greeted him as "our baby" and "our star"; he was described as the first emperor who was admired by everyone in "all the world, from the rising to the setting sun".[*] Caligula was loved for being the son of Germanicus, and for not being Tiberius. Over 160,000 animals were sacrificed during three months of public rejoicing; Philo describes the first seven months of Caligula's reign as utterly blissful.

---

[*]   Suetonius, *Caligula*.

He awarded bonuses to the military, consigned treason trials to the past, and recalled those who had been sent into exile. He lightened the tax burden and, ironically, criminalized sexual deviants, and put on lavish gladiatorial games.*

But things soon began to change. In October AD 37, Caligula fell dangerously ill, perhaps through poisoning. When he recovered he showed all the signs of paranoia and set about killing or exiling anyone close to him or whom he saw as a threat, including his cousin and co-heir Tiberius Gemellus. This outraged Caligula's and Gemellus's mutual grandmother Antonia Minor who is said to have committed suicide, although Caligula may have poisoned her. Suetonius says that Gemellus was taking medication for a persistent cough and that its smell was misconstrued as an antidote for poison. Caligula ordered him to commit suicide for which soldiers gave him a sword, and showed him how to use it with good effect.

He had his father-in-law Marcus Junius Silanus and his brother-in-law Marcus Lepidus executed; his uncle Claudius survived only because Caligula liked to have him as an object of derision. He insulted the memory of Augustus by alleging that his mother was actually conceived as the result of an incestuous relationship between Augustus and his daughter Julia the Elder.

In AD 38 Drusilla died of a fever. She had always been Caligula's favourite sister, and her death affected him badly. Hereafter, his attitude towards the surviving sisters Livilla and Agrippina cooled markedly; Caligula was replaced in their beds by his catamite friends. In AD 39 the two sisters devised a plot to assassinate him, with the help of Drusilla's widower and their cousin, Marcus Aemilius Lepidus. This became known as 'The Plot of the Three Daggers'. The plot failed, and the three conspirators were accused of treason. At Lepidus's trial, Caligula denounced Agrippina and Livilla and produced spurious letters, supposedly written by them, revealing their murder plot. Lepidus was executed by having his throat cut, while the two sisters were exiled to the Pontian Islands, Pontia and Pandateria, the third generation of imperial women to be punished in this way.

Inconsistency and unpredictability in behaviour and policy continued to increase when he restored democratic elections but continued to authorize executions without trial and forced his ally Macro to commit suicide.

Seneca the Younger delivers a fusillade on Caligula's casual, atrocious behaviour in his *De Ira*: "Gaius Caesar flogged and tortured Sextus Papinius, whose father was a consul, Betilienas Bassus, his own quaestor, and several others, both senators and knights, on the same day, not to carry out any judicial inquiry, but merely to amuse himself. Indeed, so impatient was he of any delay in receiving the pleasure which his monstrous cruelty never delayed in asking, that when walking with some ladies and

---

* Philo of Alexandria, *On the Embassy to Gaius.*

senators in his mother's gardens, along the walk between the colonnade and the river, he struck off some of their heads by lamplight ... how very small a favour it would have been to wait until morning, and not to kill the Roman people's senators in his slippers?

"How haughtily his cruelty was exercised ... he beat senators with rods; he did it so often that he made men able to say, 'It is the custom.' He tortured them with all the most dismal engines in the world, with the cord, the boots, the rack, the fire, and the sight of his own face. Even to this we may answer, 'To tear three senators to pieces with stripes and fire like criminal slaves was no such great crime for one who had thoughts of butchering the entire Senate, who was wont to wish that the Roman people had but one neck, that he might concentrate into one day and one blow all the wickedness which he divided among so many places and times. Was there ever anything so unheard-of as an execution in the night-time? Highway robbery seeks for the shelter of darkness, but the more public an execution is, the more power it has as an example and lesson. Here I shall be met by: 'This, which you are so surprised at, was the daily habit of that monster; this was what he lived for, watched for, sat up at night for.' Certainly one could find no one else who would have ordered all those whom he condemned to death to have their mouths closed by a sponge being fastened in them, that they might not have the power even of uttering a sound. What dying man was ever forbidden to groan? He feared that the last agony might find too free a voice, that he might hear what would displease him. He knew, moreover, that there were countless crimes, with which none but a dying man would dare to reproach him. When sponges were not forthcoming, he ordered the wretched men's clothes to be torn up, and the rags stuffed into their mouths. What savagery was this? Let a man draw his last breath: give room for his soul to escape through: let it not be forced to leave the body through a wound. It becomes tedious to add to this that in the same night he sent centurions to the houses of the executed men and made an end of their fathers also, that is to say, being a compassionate-minded man, he set them free from sorrow: for it is not my intention to describe the ferocity of Gaius, but the ferocity of anger, which does not merely vent its rage upon individuals, but rends in pieces whole nations, and even lashes cities, rivers, and things which have no sense of pain."

All Caligula's largesse had to be paid for, and a financial crisis followed in AD 38 and 39. Desperate fiscal measures included false accusations, finings and the killing of individuals in order to seize their estates; imposing taxes on lawsuits, weddings and prostitution; auctioning the lives of the gladiators at shows and appropriating war booty from veterans. According to Suetonius, in the first year of Caligula's reign he salted away 2.7 billion sesterces; an achievement which his nephew Nero Caesar, later emperor, envied and admired.

Erratic and eccentric behaviour continued apace: a famine occurred when Caligula seized grain boats for a pontoon bridge project; this fantastic bridge extended for over two miles from Baiae to Puteoli and was a bid to rival the Persian king Xerxes's pontoon bridge over the Hellespont. Caligula, who could not swim, would ride his horse, Incitatus, across wearing the breastplate of Alexander the Great—a retort to the prediction by Tiberius's soothsayer Thrasyllus of Mendes that Caligula had "no more chance of becoming emperor than of riding a horse across the Bay of Baiae".

He alienated and insulted the Senate when he replaced the consul and executed several senators whom he suspected of conspiring against him; others he humiliated by forcing them to wait on him and run alongside his chariot. An apparent invasion of Britannia was aborted when he ordered his troops to collect seashells as "spoils of the sea". In AD 40, Caligula started to deliberately confuse religion with politics when he began appearing in public dressed as various gods such as Hercules, Mercury, Venus and Apollo. He would refer to himself as a god in official meetings and was referred to as 'Jupiter' in state papers. He had the heads removed from various statues of gods in Rome and replaced them with his own.

Apart from routinely sleeping with his sisters and prostituting them to other men, Caligula is accused of seducing the wives of other men and of killing at a whim. Once, while attending the games, to alleviate his boredom, because there were no prisoners available, he allegedly ordered his guards to throw a section of the audience into the arena during the intermission to be eaten by the wild beasts. He sent troops on point-less military exercises, made his horse Incitatus a consul and appointed the horse as a priest. He opened a brothel in his palace, setting apart a number of rooms and furnishing them to suit the grandeur of the place, where *matronae* and freeborn youths should stand exposed. Then he sent his pages around the forums and basilicas, to invite young men and old to enjoy themselves, lending money on interest to those who came and having clerks openly take down their names, as contributors to Caesar's revenues.

In 40 AD, Caligula informed the Senate of his intentions to leave Rome permanently and to move to Alexandria, where he might be worshipped as a living god. This was too much for an already disaffected senate. Caligula did not survive for much longer. He, Milonia Caesonia, and their daughter, Julia Drusilla, were murdered outside the theatre they were attending in January AD 41, in a conspiracy led by Cassius Chaerea. Little Julia's brains were dashed out against a wall. Caligula's uncle, Claudius, was found cowering behind a curtain by a faction of the Praetorian Guard and was declared Emperor of Rome.

To what can we attribute Caligula's erratic and at times deranged and cruel behaviour? It is convenient just to write him off as insane, and this certainly serves those many writers—from contemporary times to the present day—and film-makers who offer a one-dimensional, salacious and sensational picture of the man. On a more scholarly level, Anthony Barrett points to the prevalent 19th-century (predominantly) German view that "he was more than just nervous and excitable, but that he was in fact a totally deranged lunatic, so depraved and cruel that his actions could not be judged by the norms of human behaviour. The most celebrated study of this type is *Caligula: Eine studie der römische Cäsarwahnsinn* (1894) by Ludwig Quidde."

But there is no clinical evidence for this diagnosis. Encephalitis, epilepsy, hyperthyroidism or meningitis have all been posited as possible causes or triggers for his incorrigible and unpredictable behaviour. His obsession with the moon may be accounted for by epilepsy which has lunar associations while his inability to swim may be a result of the advice given to epileptics not to swim in open waters in case of a seizure. Indeed, we must share Barrett's caution that many of the monstrous actions attributed to Caligula (and Nero) are "part and parcel of the standard profile of the stock tyrant".

Valeria Messalina (c. AD 20–48)

Horace famously called Cleopatra VII *a fatale monstrum*, a doom monster. Messalina was a *monstrum* of a different type: she was a veritable sex monster. Valeria Messalina was the third wife of Claudius, paternal cousin of Nero, second cousin of Caligula, and great-grandniece of Augustus. Claudius declined the Senate's offer to honour Messalina with the title of Augusta; fifty years later, Juvenal alluded to this when he described Messalina as "the whore Augusta" (*meretrix Augusta*), itself an allusion to Propertius's description of Cleopatra as the "whore queen" (*meretrix regina*). To Dio, Messalina was little more than "an adulteress and harlot ... for in addition to her shameless behaviour in general, she at times sat as a prostitute in the imperial palace, and compelled other women of the highest rank to do the same".

It was not long into her marriage to Claudius before a very insecure Messalina began her campaign to eliminate potential obstacles to her son's succession. That son was Britannicus. The first to go was Pompeius Magnus (AD 30–47), the husband of Claudius's daughter Antonia, who was stabbed while in bed with a favourite catamite. Messalina then ordered the execution of the celebrated Decimus Velerius Asiaticus, lauded as the first Gaul to win a consulship. He was the husband of Lollia Saturnia, the sister of Caligula's third wife, Lollia Paulina; his immense wealth allowed him to purchase and develop the sumptuous gardens of Lucullus, the renowned general, politician, and gourmet. Messalina coveted these gardens, and was similarly motivated by jealousy towards the beautiful Poppaea Sabina (the mother of Nero's wife), with whom Asiaticus was having an affair. Sabina was also a rival to Messalina's own affections for Mnester, the famous Greek dancer. Asiaticus was arrested by Publius

Suillius Rufus while holidaying in Baiae, and was accused of adultery with Poppaea, bribing the army (therefore treason) and, worst of all, effeminacy, the humiliating and derogatory opposite of *virtus*, that true badge of Roman manhood. Messalina was able to persuade Claudius that executing Asiaticus was the only option; Asiaticus duly opened his veins, concluding resignedly that he was the victim of "a woman's guile" (*fraus muliebris*). Poppaea committed suicide soon afterwards.

The elimination of Asiaticus—without trial— was a serious miscalculation on Messalina's part. This, alongside the animosity aroused by the greedy bullying of Suillius and the order to exile Polybius, won the empress no friends and considerable unpopularity. Polybius was one of Claudius's freedmen, a reliable and faithful researcher; he was eventually executed for alleged crimes against the state, trumped up by Messalina when he outstayed his welcome as a lover. On the other hand, Lucius Vitellius, an ally of Agrippina the Younger's, managed to attach himself to the court of Claudius.

Suetonius tells the strange story of Vitellius's shoe fetish: he would beg Messalina to allow him to remove her shoes, whereupon he would secrete one of them in his clothing, removing it from time to time to kiss it. This was not Vitellius's only paraphilia; he was also in the habit of mixing the saliva of a freedwoman mistress with honey, before using it as a lotion for his neck and throat.

Messalina's greatest and most bizarre *faux pas*, however, was her bigamous marriage to Gaius Silius (b. c. AD 13) in AD 48, and then allowing the discovery of the couple's plot to kill Claudius to be discovered. According to Tacitus—who was himself astonished by the fantasy of it all—her adulterous affairs had become so routine and casual that she drifted, trance-like, into "unheard-of lust". Messalina forced Silius to divorce his wife, Junia Silana. The lavish wedding of Messalina and Silius was marked by "prodigious infamy" complete with a bridal gown, witnesses, sacrifices, a wild Bacchanalia of a party, and breakfast. It all took place while an oblivious Claudius, still legally her husband, was at Ostia. The disarmingly naïve plan was for Silius to adopt Britannicus, so that he and Messalina could rule on behalf of her son until he came of age; he was then aged seven. Tiberius Claudius Narcissus exposed their sham marriage and their plot to kill Claudius, using two of Claudius's mistresses, Calpurnia and Cleopatra, as messengers. Narcissus was another of Claudius's freedmen, and wielded great influence in the imperial court. Like other freedmen, Narcissus would have been particularly stung and unnerved by the treatment meted out to Polybius; Messalina's clumsy machinations inevitably lost her the invaluable support of the freedmen surrounding the emperor.

Meanwhile, furniture and possessions were streaming out of the imperial palace destined for Silius's house, while an infatuated Messalina showered him with gifts.

The partying and fantasy came to an abrupt end, however, when Messalina realized that she had been betrayed by Narcissus. Claudius reacted to the news of the coup with incredulity, asking repeatedly if he was still emperor. Understandably, he was both incandescent and intractable. In desperation, Messalina invoked her children and enlisted the support of Vibidia—the influential chief Vestal Virgin—who demanded that she be allowed to plead her case. The farce was heightened further when Messalina attempted to forestall the returning emperor and win sympathy by hitching a lift on a cart full of garden rubbish. Of course, the cuckolded Claudius was having none of it, although, under pressure from Vibidia, he promised Messalina that he would attend to the matter the following day, while she reflected on the enormity of her stupidity and cupidity in the appropriated gardens of Lucullus.

By now Claudius was "on fire, exploding with threats". The guard was briefed, and proceeded to arrest and execute Silius and other complicit *equites*. Mnester, in an attempt to escape any blame, showed Claudius's men the whip marks from Messalina's flagellation, but was not spared: after all, he was a dancer, *histrio*, and how could a dancer be pardoned when so many illustrious men were dying? Likewise, Sextus Traulus Montanus who one night had suffered the indignity of being summoned for sex and then immediately dismissed by a capricious Messalina, was also executed. Perversely, Suilius Caesonius was spared because Messalina had forced him to play the role of a woman in a squalid orgy. Claudius presumably thought that he had suffered enough.

Messalina was joined in the gardens by her mother, Domitia Lepida the Younger—this was an extraordinary act of *pietas* (piety) and matronly behaviour on her part, considering the gulf that had divided them for many years. Desperate and angry letters were written, while copious amounts of wine helped Claudius to calm down and adopt a more lenient attitude to his remorseful wife—he was now describing her sympathetically as "the poor woman"; anger was now giving way to *amor*, and the fear, according to Tacitus, was that he would submit to "memories of the conjugal bed"

Narcissus saw this and realized that the whole affair could rebound on him. He moved quickly; Claudius's soldiers arrived in the gardens, Domitia Lepida advised her daughter to commit suicide. Messalina did not have the courage, and botched the attempt; she was then run through with a soldier's sword. Claudius received the news while dining and reacted with indifference, continuing his feast. Suetonius, to illustrate Claudius's "absent-mindedness and myopia", adds that Claudius actually asked where Messalina was when she failed to turn up for dinner that night.

Above and right: Messalina whore emperess by Eugène Cyrille Brunet (1828–1921). (Museum of Fine Arts of Rennes/ Caroline Léna Becker)

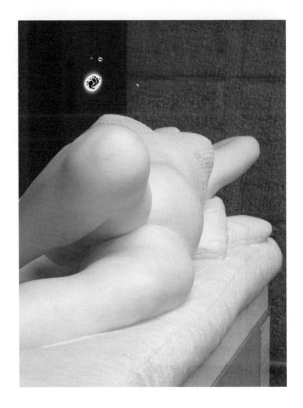

Juvenal is savagely censorious of Messalina, and must take some of the responsibility for the scandalous reception Messalina has endured down the ages. Pliny the Elder, who was less cynical and possibly more objective, also had his part to play, as of course did Tacitus and Dio. Messalina was easy prey for Juvenal; to him, she was

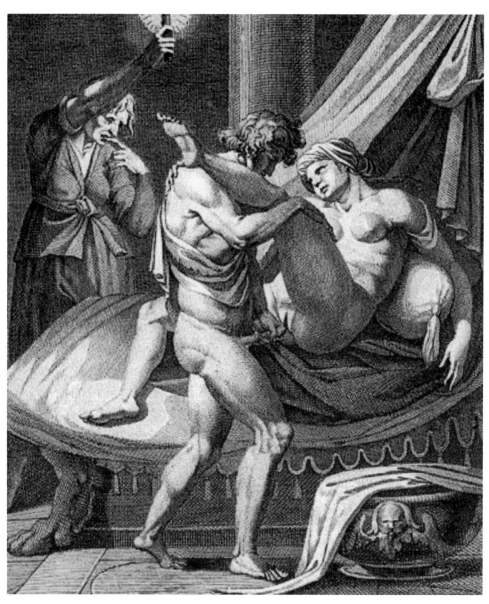

Messalina, serving as a prostitute under the pseudonym of Lysisca by Agostino Carracci (1557–1602).

the *meretrix Augusta*, stealing out of the imperial bedchamber, while Claudius slept, for a night on her back on a mat in a brothel. According to Juvenal, she wore a hood and a blonde wig to conceal her familiar, recognizable black hair, and checked into her personal cell in a fetid whorehouse. There she prostituted herself, using the working name 'Lycisca' (Wolf Bitch). She stuck out her belly, indicating "The stomach you were in, noble Britannicus". Juvenal states that Messalina was always the last of the girls to leave, staying until the very last minute, with "her clitoris still burning and stiff with lust"; to Juvenal, the clitoral erection betrayed Messalina's penis envy. She may have been worn out by the men, Juvenal records, but she still went home unsated, taking the stench of the brothel back to the imperial bed with her.

In *Satire* 10, Juvenal revisits Messalina in a reference to her sham marriage to Silius and the Catch-22 decision he had to make: refuse the marriage and he would die, but to accept was also a death sentence. Pliny the Elder gives us the unedifying story of Messalina's epic orgy, in which she challenged a veteran prostitute to a twenty-four-hour sex marathon. The empress won with a score of twenty-five partners—an average of just under one client per hour. The context in which this appears is an expatiation on the mating of animals, and Pliny's revelation that man is the only animal to which copulation is insatiable. Messalina's victory provides the evidence. Tacitus lists twelve of her distinguished equestrian lovers, who paid for their lust with their lives. Dio describes Messalina's group-sex sessions, attended by the husbands of the women involved; those who complied were rewarded, but those who declined to prostitute their wives were murdered. Messalina concealed these orgies from Claudius by providing a ready supply of slave women for his bed.

Nero (AD 37–AD 68)

Nero Claudius Caesar Augustus Germanicus had not only his great-uncle Claudius (r. AD 41–54) to thank for his elevation to the imperial throne when he adopted him and made him heir, but also his formidable mother Agrippina the Younger who worked tirelessly and ruthlessly to ensure that Nero succeeded. Agrippina was granddaughter of Augustus, younger sister of Caligula, and the niece and fourth wife of Claudius.

Claudius was a great-nephew of Augustus through his sister Octavia Minor, a nephew of Tiberius through his father Drusus, Tiberius's brother, an uncle of Caligula and a great-uncle of Nero through Caligula's father and Nero's grandfather Germanicus, his brother. Nero was the only son of Gnaeus Domitius Ahenobarbus and Agrippina the Younger. His maternal grandparents were Germanicus and Agrippina the Elder. His mother was one of Caligula's sisters. He was Augustus' great-great-grandson, descended from the first emperor's only daughter Julia.

Statue of Nero as a boy, 1st century AD. (Prioryman)

AGRIPPINA THE YOUNGER (AD 15–59) was granddaughter of Augustus, younger sister of Caligula, and the niece and fourth wife of Claudius. Agrippina saw her chance to murder Claudius and install Nero, her son, on the imperial throne: the only question was the type of poison to use. Anxious that Claudius might recant on his death bed and rehabilitate Britannicus if a slow-working

Agrippina crowns her son Nero with a laurel wreath. She carries a cornucopia, symbol of fortune and plenty, and he wears the armour and cloak of a Roman commander, with a helmet on the ground at his feet. The scene refers to Nero's accession as emperor in AD 54 and belongs before AD 59 when Nero had Agrippina murdered. (Aphrodisias Museum, Turkey/ Carlos Delgado)

poison was used and aware that an aggressive, instantaneous toxin would be incriminating, she compromised with a venom that would drive him insane before delivering a slow death. Locusta, a woman proficient in pharmacology with a criminal conviction hanging over her head for poisoning, *veneficii damnata*, was enlisted. The poison was prepared; it was to be administered by a eunuch, Halotus, a regular dish taster. Tacitus says that a particularly juicy mushroom was smeared with the poison but failed to be effective: a terrified Agrippina called in Claudius's physician, Gaius Stertinius Xenophon, who was in on the plot, so that he could introduce a poisoned feather into Claudius's throat, pretending to make

him vomit. Suetonius, too, subscribes to the mushroom theory telling how Nero later quoted the Greek proverb which describes mushrooms as the "food of the gods" (*cibus deorum*). What exactly killed Claudius is open to speculation; fungi, of course, are unpredictable things and it may be that Claudius died of an accidental poisoning, malaria or natural causes. Whatever, Nero, her sixteen-year-old son, was now Emperor of Rome.

Claudius was not the only victim of Agrippina's obsession with elevating Nero: others included Domitia Lepida, Nero's aunt; Marcus Junius Silanus, a great-grandson of Augustus; and Tiberius Claudius Narcissus, one of Claudius' freedmen in charge of correspondence (*praepositus ab epistulis*).

Agrippina the Younger by Aegidius Sadeler II. (Achenbach Foundation for Graphic Arts, San Francisco)

Due in no small part to the tabloid biographer Suetonius, the picture we have of Nero is of a man who, like Caligula before him, was mad and unremittingly cruel. While there is without doubt some truth in this, it is, as with Caligula, not the entire picture. When Agrippina was exiled by Caligula with Julia Livilla, Nero was disinherited and sent to live with his paternal aunt Domitia Lepida, the mother of Claudius's third wife Valeria Messalina. When he reached the age of sixteen, Nero married Claudius's daughter Claudia Octavia, his own step-sister.

As with Caligula, Nero's extravagant building programme left Rome in financial crisis. As with Caligula he naïvely attempted to clean up the political situation, to drain the swamp, by ending secret trials, to eradicate corruption and political nepotism, and to respect the privileges of the Senate and individual senators. Just as naïve was his plan to abolish taxes in AD 58.

History seemed to be repeating itself when, just as Livia fell out irrevocably with her son Tiberius, then so did Agrippina with Nero. A freedwoman called Claudia Acte was the catalyst for the rift between Nero and his mother. Nero much preferred this exciting young girl, who satisfied his adulterous desires, to his noble and virtuous wife Octavia, whom he had grown to despise. At the same time, to make the situation worse, two fashionable young men-about-town started to insinuate themselves into Nero's life: Marcus Salvius Otho (a future emperor) and Claudius Senecio.

Tacitus tells us that when Agrippina found out about Acte, she predictably raged as only a jealous woman or an over-protective mother can, incensed at having to compete with a former slave girl and at the prospect of having a lowly maid as her daughter-in-law. The nastier his mother's reproaches, the more Nero burned with love for Acte, until the power of that love began to turn him against Agrippina. He took solace in Seneca and Annaeus Serenus, who had been complicit in Nero's affair from the start, even to the extent that Serenus had posed as Acte's lover in order to divert suspicion. Nero was so besotted with Acte that at some point during their three-year affair he expressed a desire to marry her; in a feeble public relations exercise he fabricated a family tree which showed how her ancestry was linked with King Attalus of Pergamum, bribing some ex-consuls to swear to her royal birth right. Agrippina soon realized the futility of her inflexibility and adopted a more indulgent and generous approach. She offered Nero and Acte the use of her bedroom, plied him with gifts, and admitted that her earlier severity had been intemperate.

Too late: Agrippina was now isolated, and easy prey to anyone seeking revenge. One such predator was Junia Silana. She was later embroiled in Messalina's plot to murder Claudius, and was forced to divorce her husband, Gaius Silius. Junia was noted for her lineage, her looks, and her lascivious behaviour—*insignis genere forma lascivia*—and had once been a friend of Agrippina's. However, this friendship soured when Agrippina did Junia no favours when she deterred the noble, eligible Titus Sextius Aficanus from marrying Junia—Agrippina gossiped that Junia was a loose woman, and 'past it' (*impudicam et vergentem annis dictitans*). Tacitus says that Agrippina had no designs on Africanus herself, but rather she was trying to keep her friend, the childless (and heirless) wealthy widow out of the grasp of an obvious bounty hunter—probably because she had an eye on Junia's legacy herself.

Junia did not appreciate Agrippina's uncharacteristic altruism, and saw her chance for revenge. Her plot entailed accusing Agrippina of inciting Rubellius Plautus, son of Tiberius' granddaughter Julia, to overthrow Nero, marrying him, making Plautus emperor and taking over Rome together. Paris, a regular and usually jovial visitor to Nero's chamber at that time of night, was deputed to tell Nero this sorry tale. Nero was terrified; his immediate reaction was to murder Agrippina and Plautus and remove Burrus, a noted ally of his mother's, from his position as head of the Praetorian Guard. The distraught and frightened Nero was keen to kill his mother—*trepidus et interficiendae matris avidus*—but others, Seneca and Burrus in particular, advised caution: Agrippina would indeed be executed if found guilty but she must be allowed, and seen, to defend herself; moreover, there was only one accuser in the case and he was not particularly reliable: put another way, it was late, they had enjoyed a convivial evening and it was all getting a bit rash and silly: *omniaque temeritati et inscitiae propiora.*

Agrippina got her defence: Burra and Seneca visited Agrippina the following morning and read the charges for her to deny, or confess and suffer the penalty. She responded with her usual ferocity, *ferocia*, demanding to know how Junia could possibly know what a mother feels, stating that parents do not change their children as often as disreputable women like Junia change their adulterous men. She proceeded then to discredit all the guilty parties, winning Nero's permission to reward her supporters and wreak vengeance on her accusers. Paris, however, escaped punishment: he was too good a player in Nero's nocturnal debaucheries. Altogether, a remarkable display of Agrippina's power over Nero, even at a time when the relationship between mother and son was at its lowest ebb.

In AD 58, Agrippina and Rome were threatened by another *impudicitia* (lit. impurity) in the person of Poppaea Sabina. Tacitus tells us that she was woman who had everything—everything, that is, apart from honesty. She inherited glory and good looks from her exceptionally beautiful mother; she was rich, and a *docta puella* (*sermo comis nec absurdum ingenium*), literally a girl who made polite conversation. She preached modesty (*modestia*) but practised salaciousness (*lascivia*). She was something of a recluse, but when she did go out she wore a veil, either to tantalize men or to accentuate the allure of her beauty. She cared nothing for her reputation, and made no distinction between married men and adulterers; she never lost control of herself, and she was never controlled by a man. Where there was a chance of personal advancement, her lust came to the fore. Nero composed a poem that celebrated her striking auburn hair, triggering a fashion among the women of Rome. Her predilection for bathing in asses' milk also started a craze, as did 'Poppaea's Cream', an anti-ageing lotion which eradicated wrinkles. According to Dio, Poppaea really believed it when someone told her that in milk "lurked a magic which would dispel all diseases and blights from her beauty".

Poppaea was first married to Rufinius Crispinus; they had a son together. She later had an affair with the libertine Otho, Nero's very good friend, which ended in divorce for Crispinus and marriage to Otho. Tactlessly and annoyingly for the emperor, Otho would praise Poppaea to Nero, ever reminding him of her beauty and elegance (*forma elegantiaque*), endlessly going on about her nobility and fine looks (*dictitans nobilitatem pulchritudinem*). Inevitably this only served to forge a link between Poppaea and Nero, and an affair ensued. She coquettishly led him on, coaxing him, "I'm a married woman; you still love Acte, your serving concubine." He grew more and more frustrated. Poppaea emphasized the difference between her fine lifestyle, with her one-of-a-kind husband Otho, and Nero's grubby, low-life, servile relationship with Acte. Otho was soon removed from the scene, posted to a governorship in far-off Lusitania to contemplate his tactlessness.

The following year, in AD 59, Nero's passion for Poppaea grew all the more intense. She had hopes of marrying the emperor, but realized that this was unrealistic while Agrippina was still around; she accused him of being under his mother's thumb. An artful adulteress, she cited her own beauty, lineage, fertility and sincerity in contrast to his mother's arrogance and greed. Poppaea's aim was to persuade Nero to assassinate his mother, and then marry her. According to Dio, Seneca also urged Nero to commit matricide.

Agrippina was not to be outdone. Tacitus records how Cluvius relates that Agrippina, in a bid to compete and maintain her influence, would dress up provocatively at around midday and offer up her body to Nero, already drunk by that time of day. However, the lascivious kisses and shameful caresses did not go unnoticed; Seneca enlisted Acte's help, believing that only a woman could help against another woman's blandishments. Acte told Nero that his disgraceful incest was public knowledge, that Agrippina was glorying in spreading it about, and, crucially, that his behaviour was weakening his position with the Praetorian Guard. Rumour had it that Agrippina and Nero had sex every time they shared a litter, proven by the state their clothes were in when they emerged. Suetonius adds that Agrippina was later deterred from further incest with Nero by her enemies, who gossiped that having sexual relations with him would only make him harder to tame and more despotic (*ferox atque impotens mulier*).

Nero was oblivious. His reaction was to find another woman who looked exactly like his mother, a surrogate mother. He found one and, according to Dio, "when he toyed with the girl herself or displayed her charms to others, he would say that he was wont to have intercourse with his mother".

By now Agrippina, perhaps fearing the worst, began to spend more time at her villas outside Rome at Tusculum and Antium. Clearly Nero had had enough of his turbulent mother and was now determined to murder her, the only question being whether it be by poison, sword or some other violent means. Like Tiberius before him, he had threatened to abdicate and go into exile, on Rhodes. He had her pestered with irritating law suits and he hired mobs to jeer loudly and insultingly outside her house. But the feeble anti-social behaviour was all to no avail. Any plot was fraught with problems; poisoning was not an option due to Agrippina's paranoid but prudent habit of taking prophylactic antidotes against poisons.

Shipwreck and sabotage were the solution. Anicetus, commander of the fleet at Misenum, came up with the ingenious idea of building a ship with a section which would fall away at sea and throw Agrippina overboard. Dio says that the idea was inspired by a ship Anicetus had seen in the theatre that automatically split in two, let out some animals, and then came together again, quite seaworthy. A similar vessel was built while Nero showered his mother with flattery and devotion to put her off her guard. The festival of Minerva, the Quinquatria, at Baiae was chosen as the time and place: the special boat, built in Agrippina's honour and magnificently decked out, was placed at her disposal. However, Agrippina got wind of the plot and travelled to Baiae by litter.

After an extended banquet at which a good time was had by all, Nero dutifully escorted his mother to the vessel for the return journey which she boarded with her attendants, Crepereius Gallus and Acerronia Polla. Everyone was happy that Nero and Agrippina had seemingly been reconciled. Then, at a signal, the lead-lined canopy collapsed into the boat, killing Gallus outright. Acerronia and Agrippina survived, but the boat did not sink as planned and the crew had to scuttle it. Acerronia, thinking to save her own skin, pretended to be Agrippina and screamed for help; a more ill-conceived strategy would be hard to find: she was battered to death by oars and poles wielded by those convinced she was Agrippina, while the real, injured Agrippina was able to swim to safety; she was eventually picked up by a passing boat.

Suetonius' version is even more melodramatic, and comedic: he says that Nero was irritated by his mother's overbearing behaviour and made three attempts to poison her only to be thwarted by timely antidotes. Nero then attempted to crush her with a mechanical ceiling suspended over her bed. When this failed because of a tip-off, he had a collapsible boat built on which the cabin would fall in on itself, or it would be shipwrecked when boats rammed it. In the event Agrippina sailed to Baiae in her own boat; plan B was to stage a collision in which her galley was damaged. For the return journey, a happy Nero escorted her to the quay where he kissed her breasts before she boarded the custom-built boat which had been offered on account of the damage to her own galley. Dio adds that on reaching Bauli, Nero gave a series of sumptuous banquets over several days at which he entertained his mother "with every show of friendliness ...he embraced her at the close of dinner about midnight, and straining her to his breast, kissed her eyes and hands, exclaiming: 'Strength and good health to you, mother. For you I live and because of you I rule.' Though the ship parted asunder and Agrippina fell into the water, she did not perish. Notwithstanding that it was dark and that she was glutted with strong drink and that the sailors used their oars against her with such force that they killed Acerronia Polla, her companion on the trip, she nevertheless got safely to shore."*

A detachment of armed men arrived later at Agrippina's house, broke down the door and entered her bedroom, where she waited with one maid. The maid deserted her. A delusional Agrippina, ever the dutiful son-loving mother, declared that Nero was not to blame in the boating incident, stating, "But if you have come here to commit a crime, I believe my son is not involved, he would not murder his mother" (S*in facinus patraturus, nihil se de filio credere; non imperatum parricidium*). One of the officers then smashed her on the head with a club; when another drew his sword to finish her off she shouted, "Strike my womb!" (V*entrem feri*), a dying reference to Nero. Dio is more explicit: "she knew for what they had come, and leaping up from her bed she tore open her clothing, exposing her abdomen, and cried out, 'Strike here, Anicetus, strike here, because this bore Nero!'"

Tacitus believes that some sources insisted that Nero then displayed an unhealthy interest in his mother's corpse, dashing off to look at it, fondling the limbs, finding fault with other parts, casually taking a drink when he got thirsty (*ad visendum interfectae cadaver accurrisse, contrectasse membra, alia vituperasse, sitique interim oborta bibisse*).

For Dio, the suggestions of necrophilia are more opaque, but just as sinister: "The deed was so monstrous that he was overwhelmed by incredulity; he therefore desired to behold the victim of his crime with his own eyes. So he laid bare her body, looked her all over, and inspected her wounds, finally uttering a remark far more abominable than even than even the murder. His words were: 'I did not know I had

---

* Dio says that Acerronia drowned and mentions nothing about Agrippina being rescued, and instead claims she swam all the way to shore unaided. Dio prefers a vessel where the bottom opened up while at sea; Agrippina duly fell into the water when exactly that happened.

such a beautiful mother.'" Her ghost haunted him and in a bid to rid himself of this spectre he enlisted magicians to call up her ghost and exorcise the evil.

It comes as no surprise that the omens were not good. One woman gave birth to a snake, while another was struck by lightning while she was having sex with her husband; the sun went out, and the fourteen districts of Rome were struck by lightning. Nevertheless, after a triumphant return to Rome, Tacitus tells us that Nero "then immersed himself in all sorts of debaucheries, from which hitherto a kind of respect for Agrippina had not exactly restrained him, but had modulated his behaviour".

Nero was not averse to physically abusing his wives. He had tried to strangle his first wife, Octavia, on three occasions. This politically contrived marriage bored him; he loathed her because she was popular and the daughter of an emperor, so he divorced her on the grounds that she was barren. Poppaea Sabina, however, was not satisfied with this; Tacitus tells us how she had one of Octavia's slave girls denounce Octavia for adultery with an Alexandrian flautist called Eucaerus. 'Witnesses' refused to condemn her, even under torture. One such brave witness was Pythias, a slave girl who stood up for Octavia under interrogation and torture; she defiantly spat in the face of her interrogator, Tigellinus, when he questioned Octavia's virtue, exclaiming, "My mistress's cunt [*muliebria*] is cleaner than your mouth!" This was a particularly humiliating insult for a Roman, who revered the mouth as an inviolable organ of oratory; the vagina, on the other hand, and its associations with oral sex were anathema. Octavia was banished to Campania under military guard.

A persistent Poppaea urged Nero to finish off Octavia so he bribed Anicetus to allege that he had been having an affair with that Octavia. Nero then was able to announce that Octavia had plotted to take over the fleet by seducing Anicetus, and that she had had an abortion (conveniently forgetting his charge of infertility) to hide her libidinous behaviour. Nero exiled her to Pandateria, where she was told of her impending death a few days later. Octavia invoked the name of Agrippina, but to no avail. She was tied up and her veins were cut, and to hurry things along she was placed in a very hot bath. Her head was presented to Poppaea in Rome.

Nero later kicked Poppaea to death when she was heavily pregnant; she had complained of being ill, and had the temerity to scold him for returning late from the races. Tacitus says that she was buried in the Mausoleum of Augustus; her body was not cremated (according to Roman custom), but was stuffed with spices and embalmed in the Egyptian way. One year's supply of incense was burned at the funeral.

The fallout from Poppaea's death led to yet more psychotic and unbalanced behaviour in Nero. So much did he miss Poppaea that he sought out a surrogate who resembled her—and found Sporus who was not a woman but a young man. Nero's people then castrated the ex-slave and the couple married. Sporus joined Nero in bed with

Pythagoras, who nightly played the role of husband in their troilism. Sporus routinely accompanied Nero, decked out as his empress, even making one of his favourites, the powerful Calvia Crispinilla—Tacitus calls her Nero's "tutor in vice" (*magistrate libidinum*)—Sporus's "mistress of wardrobe". A disgusted Tacitus has left us his thoughts on the earlier wedding between Nero's wine servant, Pythagoras, and Nero: "He stooped to marry himself to one of that filthy herd, by name Pythagoras, with all the forms of regular wedlock. The bridal veil was put over the emperor; people saw the witnesses of the ceremony, the wedding dower, the couch and the nuptial torches; everything in a word was plainly visible, which, even when a woman weds, darkness hides."

This all took place at the banquets of Tigellinus, where another nauseating spectacle of after-dinner entertainment took place: Nero, draped in the skins of wild animals, would be released from a cage to mutilate the genitals of men and women who were bound to stakes. He raped a Vestal Virgin, and committed incest with his mother. He dealt with annoying senators by threatening to have their wives thrown into the arena.

Antonia, Claudius's daughter, was selected to take Poppaea's place, but she refused. Her defiance led to her execution on a charge of attempting a coup. Nero raped Aulus Plautius and then killed him, declaring that Agrippina could now come and kiss his successor: Nero believed that she had conducted an affair with Plautius, and had backed him in a takeover bid for the throne. Nero had Rufrius Crispinus, Poppaea's son from an earlier marriage, killed by the boy's own slaves while he was out fishing; the pretext was that Rufrius had been playing 'generals and emperors': this was seen as treasonable.

Nero drove Seneca to suicide in AD 65, and poisoned Burrus with a toxic cough medicine. Seneca planned for his wife, Pompeia Paulina, to die with him, but she survived her suicide attempt when Nero's henchmen interceded and administered an antidote. Epicharis, a player in the Pisonian conspiracy against Nero in AD 65 excited a different kind of anxiety. An exceedingly brave freedwoman, she was informed against when trying to recruit more conspirators. Tacitus paints a picture of an insecure Nero who inflicted torture on her female body (*muliebre corpus*), and ordered the beatings, burnings and verbal assault to be intensified—so as not to be outdone by a woman (*ne a femina spernerentur*). Epicharis had the last word, though, when, crippled by the torture, in order not to betray her colleagues, she hanged herself. Tacitus ensured that his readers, and history, remembers her courage, her illustrious behaviour—and the cowardice and treachery of her co-conspirators: freeborn equestrians and senators themselves busy shamelessly informing on each other, their families and friends. A famous example is Lucan, the epic poet, selling his own mother, Acilia, to Nero's thugs.

In AD 62, and after his matricide of AD 59, Nero arranged for the first treason (*maiestas*) trial of his reign, against Antistius Sosianus. Rivals Cornelius Sulla and Rubellius Plautus were also executed, thus signalling a much more robust attitude towards the Senate.

The Great Fire of Rome took place on the night of 18/19 July AD 64 and devastated much of the city. If Nero was behind it—Tacitus says not, Suetonius, Dio and Pliny the Elder say he was—then we can add arson to matricide, domestic abuse, necrophilia, political murder and fornication. Depending on his motives, we can perhaps add social cleansing when he used the fire to clear away thousands of houses and their occupants to make way for his lavish and extensive Domus Aurea (House of Gold); and religious intolerance when he blamed the conflagration on the Christians with many arrested and either brutally executed as live fodder for wild animals in the arena, crucified or burned alive. Nero pinned the blame on, and inflicted the most exquisite tortures against, a class hated for their abominations: Christians, or Chrestians as they were known by the populace.

The Fire of Rome as depicted by Hubert Robert in 1785. (Musée d'art moderne André Malraux/ HAHxg_lHmo6TqQ)

However, Tacitus's full account could not be more different: he believes Nero to have been in Antium at the time but he hastened back to the city to take control of a relief effort he paid for from his personal funds. He participated in the search for and rescue of victims over many days spent searching the debris, opening his palaces to provide shelter for the homeless, and arranging emergency food supplies.

As we might expect, Lucius Caecilius Firminianus Lactantius, the Christian zealot, writing in around AD 313-6—demonizes Nero: "And while Nero reigned, the Apostle Peter came to Rome, and, through the power of God committed unto him, wrought certain miracles, and, by turning many to the true religion, built up a faithful and steadfast temple unto the Lord. When Nero heard of those things, and observed that not only in Rome, but in every other place, a great multitude revolted daily from the worship of idols, and, condemning their old ways, went over to the new religion, he, an execrable and pernicious tyrant, sprung forward to raze the heavenly temple and destroy the true faith. He it was who first persecuted the servants of God; he crucified Peter, and slew Paul: nor did he escape with impunity; for God looked on the affliction of His people; and therefore the tyrant, bereaved of authority, and precipitated from the height of empire, suddenly disappeared, and even the burial-place of that noxious wild beast was nowhere to be seen. This has led some persons of extravagant imagination to suppose that, having been conveyed to a distant region, he is still reserved alive; and to him they apply the

A Christian woman is martyred in this re-enactment of the myth of Dirce by Henryk Siemiradzki (1843–1902). (National Museum Warsaw)

'Nero's Torches' or 'Christian Candlesticks' by Henryk Siemiradzki (1843–1902). (National Museum Kraków)

Sibylline verses concerning 'The fugitive, who slew his own mother, being to come from the uttermost boundaries of the earth' as if he who was the first should also be the last persecutor, and thus prove the forerunner of Antichrist! But we ought not to believe those who, affirming that the two prophets Enoch and Elias have been translated into some remote place that they might attend our Lord when He shall come to judgment, also fancy that Nero is to appear hereafter as the forerunner of the devil, when he shall come to lay waste the earth and overthrow mankind."

As for reconstruction, Nero commissioned an urban development plan which included houses less crowded and built of brick with porticos on wide roads. It was on spare land that the Domus Aurea was built. To pay for all of this he raised taxes in the provinces and devalued the currency, the first ever such devaluation in the Roman world.

A conspiracy led by Gaius Calpurnius Piso followed in AD 65; when it was exposed the usual mass executions took place, including that of Lucan, the poet. In AD 68 there was rebellion under the leadership of Gaius Julius Vindex, the governor of Gallia Lugdunensis, and Servius Sulpicius Galba, the governor of Hispania Tarraconensis. The revolt was quelled but Galba's star was in the ascendent: Nero accepted his fate and attempted suicide. He failed unstoically and forced his private secretary, Epaphroditos, to deliver the final blow. Nero bled to death and with him died the Julio-Claudian dynasty. Galba succeeded, briefly, and in so doing, initiated the Flavian Dynasty.

Right: Jacques-Louis David's 1799 depiction of a Sabine woman. (Louvre)

Below left: Wilhelm von Plüschow's 1906 work entitled 'The Christian Martyr'; apparently homoeroticism was not restricted to the Romans.

Below right: Anthoni Schoonjans' interpretation of the Vestal Virgins.

Early Christian worship in the Catacombs of Saint Calixtus, c. AD 50.

Right: Saints Abdon and Sennen bury
the remains of Christian martyrs, by
Guillaume Courtois.

Below: The Christian virgins being
exposed to the populace, by Felix
Ressureccion Hidalgo, 1884.

An orgy on Capri during the reign of Tiberius, by Henryk Siemiradzki, 1881.

Horace and Lydia, by Thomas Couture c. 1843. The subjects of this painting have traditionally been identified as the Roman poet, Quintus Horatius Flaccus (65–8 BC) and Lydia, a Roman courtesan, who figures prominently in the poet's *Odes*. An identical composition, though distinguished by more dramatic illumination, is in the Wallace collection, London, inv. P340, dated 1843, listed as 'A Roman Feast'. (Walters Art Museum)

Vitellius (AD 15–69)

"... stained with every kind of lascivious debauchery"

Suetonius, *Vitellius*

Vitellius—Aulus Vitellius Germanicus Augustus—was emperor for eight months, from 16 April to 22 December 69. He was proclaimed emperor following the quick succession of the previous emperors Galba and Otho, in the Year of the Four Emperors.

Vitellius had the dubious fortune to have been one of Tiberius's young boys in his den of iniquity on Capri; there he met Caligula with whom he became friends. He is famous for a number of unsavoury things: his predilection for and expertise at pederasty, his gluttony and his shoe and foot fetish. Never one for discipline, Vitellius marched on Rome at the head of an army intent on rape, murder and plunder; the Senate accepted him and in so doing turned their city into a scene of Bacchanalian riot and butchery with gladiatorial shows and extravagant feasting. Vitellius disbanded the existing Praetorian Guard and installed his own men in their place. Neither was he one for public relations: he is aid to have declared, "Only one thing smells better to me than a dead enemy and that's a dead fellow citizen."

He murdered his son Petronianus, who was blind in one eye, from his first marriage to wife Petronia: the spurious charge was that he had attempted parricide, and

Romans during the Decadence by Thomas Couture (1815–1879) in 1847. (Musée d'Orsay)

Vitellius dragged through the streets of Rome by the people by Georges Rochegrosse (1859–1938) in 1883. (Palazzo Nuovo, Musei Capitolini, Rome/ José Luiz Bernardes Ribeiro)

that his guilty conscience led him to drink the poison which he had mixed for his intended crime.

Excessively indolent and morbidly obese, Vitellius's prodigious gluttony is legendary: he would routinely eat four banquets a day indulging in rare foods sourced and brought to him by the Roman navy. Ironically, it is reported that he starved his own mother to death— in fulfilment of a prophecy that his rule would be longer if his mother predeceased him; an alternative report has it that his mother asked for poison with which to commit suicide, a request he gladly granted. Both had had enough of each other.

Suetonius gives us some detail: breakfast, lunch, dinner and a drinking bout; and he was readily able to do justice to all of them through his habit of taking emetics. Moreover, he had himself invited to each of these meals by different men on the same day, and the materials for any one of them never cost less than 400,000 sesterces. Most notorious of all was the dinner given by his brother to celebrate his arrival in Rome, at which 2,000 of the choicest fishes and 7,000 birds are said to have been served. He himself eclipsed even this at the dedication of a platter, which on account of its enormous size he called the 'Shield of Minerva, Defender of the City'. In this he mingled the livers of pike, the brains of pheasants and peacocks, the tongues of flamingos and the milt of lampreys, brought by his captains and triremes from the whole empire, from Parthia to the Spanish strait. Being besides a man of an appetite that was not only boundless, but also regardless of time or decency, he could never refrain, even when sacrificing or making a journey, from snatching bits of meat and cakes amid the altars, almost from the very fire, and devouring them on the spot; and in the cook shops along the road, viands smoking hot or even those left over from the day before and partly consumed.

His cruelty was just as repellent; Suetonius again: "He delighted in inflicting death and torture on anyone whatsoever and for any cause whatever, putting to death several men of rank, fellow students and comrades of his, whom he had solicited to come to court by every kind of deception, all but offering them a share in the rule. This he did in various treacherous ways, even giving poison to one of them with his own hand in a glass of cold water, for which the man had called when ill of a fever. Besides he spared hardly one of the money-lenders, contractors, and tax-gatherers who had ever demanded of him the payment of a debt at Rome or of a toll on a journey.

When one of these had been handed over for execution just as he was paying his morning call and at once recalled, as all were praising the emperor's mercy, Vitellius gave orders to have him killed in his presence, saying that he wished to feast his eyes. In another case he had two sons who attempted to intercede for their father put to death with [their father]. A Roman knight also, who cried as he was being taken off to execution, 'You are my heir', he compelled to show his will; and reading that one

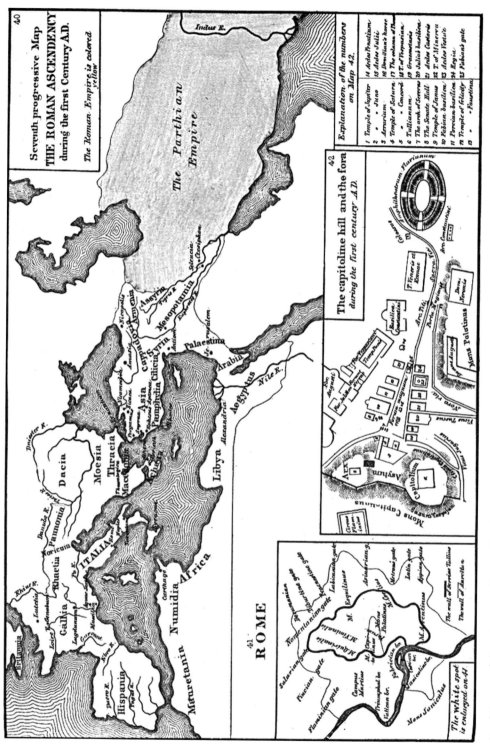

An 1884 map of the 1st century Roman Empire.

of the man's freedmen was put down as joint-heir with himself, he ordered the death both of the knight and the freedman. He even killed some of the common people, merely because they had openly spoken ill of the Blue faction, saying that they had ventured to do this from contempt of himself and the anticipation of a change of rulers. But he was especially hostile to writers of lampoons and to astrologers, and whenever any one of them was accused, he put him to death without trial."

Before he forced him to commit suicide, Vitellius humiliated Sporus, the catamite of Nero, Sabinus and Otho, by having him play the part of a girl who had been raped—the ultimate shame for a Roman.

In the end, when Vespasian, his successor, came calling, Vitellius was hauled out of a hiding place and dragged to the Gemonian stairs down which he was shoved. His body was thrown into the Tiber according to Suetonius; Cassius Dio says that Vitellius was beheaded and his head paraded around Rome.

Domitian (AD 51–96)

"He [Domitian] used to say that the lot of Emperors was most unfortunate, since when they discovered a conspiracy, no one believed them unless they had been murdered."

Suetonius, *Domitian 21*

Bust of Domitian; an antique head with body added in the 18th century. (Musée du Louvre, Paris/ Photographersailko)

Titus Flavius Caesar Domitianus Augustus reigned from AD 81 to 96. He was the younger brother of Titus and the son of Titus Flavius Vespasianus, his two predecessors, and the last member of the Flavian dynasty. His mother was Flavia Domitilla Maior; he had an older sister, Domitilla the Younger, and a brother, also called Titus Flavius Vespasianus. His reign is characterized by the authoritarian, despotic control he brought to bear over the Senate, considerably reducing their powers.

The picture we get of Domitian from establishment authors Tacitus, Pliny the Younger and Suetonius is of an egregious and paranoid tyrant; however, this may be seen as a politically biased and selective view; in reality it might be argued that ruthless and autocratic he indeed was but his cultural, economic, and political agendas laid the basis for the relatively peaceful second century which followed his reign. Domitian saw himself as the new Augustus, an enlightened tyrant with a mission to take the Roman Empire into a new golden age. His religious, military and cultural propaganda machine engendered a personality cult, and by voting himself perpetual censor, he was able to control public and private morals; Domitian was popular with the people and the army, but considered a tyrant by the Senate.

According to Suetonius the imperial bureaucracy never ran more efficiently than under Domitian, whose micromanagement, obsessive over-curiosity in minutiae, and robust standards led to an all-time low level of nepotism and corruption among provincial governors and state officials. There were, of course, unfortunate and terrible casualties: prosecutions for corruption among public officials increased, freedom of speech was restricted, libel was punished by exile or death and informers, *delatores,* flourished, feeding Domitian's naturally superstitious nature and bringing about countless false charges of treason.

By the age of sixteen Domitian's mother and sister had long been dead, while his father and brother were always away on military service in Germania and Judaea. This lonely adolescence, devoid of the security brought by close relatives, extended into his adult life when he spent long periods in solitude. As a young boy he was something of a homosexual playboy: one of his more famous affairs was with Claudius Pollo; another was with the future emperor Nerva.

Domitian was an educated, urbane and intelligent man with an ability to quote the classics at will—Homer and Virgil for example. He wrote poetry and published in law and public administration. He went bald early in life, a condition about which he was very sensitive; so obsessive was he that he took to wearing wigs and even wrote a treatise on hair care, perhaps as a form of therapy. Nevertheless, he seems to have developed a taste for habitually depilating his mistresses; he also frequently went swimming with common prostitutes.

This lonely young man cannot have helped being touched by the political turmoil of the 60s, culminating in AD 69 in the Year of the Four Emperors which brought his dynasty, the Flavians, to power and with it a period of anarchy and chaos.

In AD 70 Vespasian wanted a dynastic marriage between Domitian and his virgin niece, the daughter of Titus, Julia Flavia Titi; but Domitian was having none of it, set as he was on Domitia Longina. He even went so far as to persuade Domitia's husband, Lucius Aelius Lamia, to divorce her so that he could marry her himself. He later had Lamia executed for treason when he mentioned to Domitia, who had praised his voice, that he had given up sex and gone into training. In the meantime Domitian was only too happy to seduce Julia Flavia once she had married T. Flavius Sabinus. Domitian made her pregnant and arranged the abortion which killed her. Julia was deified and her ashes were mixed with Domitian's on his

Domitia. (Musée du Louvre/ Clio20)

death, and secretly smoked by an old nurse in the Temple of the Flavians.

In 80 Domitian and Domitia had their only child, a son who died in childhood in AD 83. That same year Domitian exiled Domitia, but soon recalled her, perhaps to scotch rumours that he was having that affair with Julia Flavia.

It is the tabloid version of events which has prevailed. According to Suetonius, Domitia Longina was exiled because of her affair with a celebrity actor named Paris. When Domitian disovered this he allegedly murdered Paris in broad daylight in the street and promptly divorced and exiled Domitia, and took Julia as his mistress; as noted she later died during an abortion. The abortion and the reason for the exile are most probably examples of historians economizing with the truth in order to vilify: her exile was more likely due to the fact that she failed to provide Domitian with an heir.

Domitian had his doubts over the moral rectitude of the Vestal Virgins: he brought a number to trial in AD 83 and AD 90 in a bid to improve the moral climate, particularly as it seemed to him that the Vestals had mislaid their moral compasses, and their virginities, under Vespasian and Titus, and were running what amounted to a brothel. In AD 83 the Oculata sisters and Varronilla were given the option to commit suicide while their lovers were exiled; seven years later, Cornelia, the Chief Virgin, was condemned to the living death that was entombment, while her lover was whipped to death.

Vesta was the goddess of the hearth, traditionally attended by virgin priestesses, the VESTAL VIRGINS, who kept the sacred flame, *ignis inextinctus*, alight in the Temple of Vesta. This flame symbolized the nourishment and health of the Roman state; the *Virgo Vestalis Maxima* symbolized the wife of old Roman kings (represented in turn by the *Pontifex Maximus*) while the others, the College, were the symbolic daughters of the king. The kings were said to originate from sparks in the ground. Any Vestal careless enough to allow the flame to go out was whipped; tending the flame occupied the Vestals for around eight hours every day. The Vestals' virginity embodied the safety of Rome: Rome was safe while their virginity remained intact; when it was violated, Rome was under threat.

The last known *vestalis maxima* was Coelia Concordia, appointed in AD 380. The Vestals were finally disbanded in AD 394 but not before ten or so had been entombed alive, the awful penalty for a Vestal who lost her virginity (*incestum*), or was suspected of having lost it. The entombment took place in a cellar under the Campus Sceleratus; the male partner was flogged to death in the Comitium like a slave, *sub furca*, or under the fork. The rationale behind

Early 18th-century depiction of the dedication of a new Vestal, by Alessandro Marchesini (1663–1738). (Hermitage Museum)

entombment was that Vesta would still be able to rescue the 'Virgin' if she were innocent. Vesta never did. Plutarch graphically describes the solemn process where the condemned Vestal is bound and gagged and carried to her subterranean prison in a curtained litter; she is unbound and, after a prayer, the Pontifex Maximus puts her on a ladder which leads to the small chamber below. The ladder is hauled up, the entrance closed and covered with earth. The chamber has a bed, lamp, bread, water, milk and oil. To Plutarch this is the most shocking spectacle in the world; when it occurs it is the most horrific day Rome has ever seen.

Vestal Virgins sometimes took the blame when catastrophe struck: for example their alleged *incestum* was held responsible for the slaughter that was the battle of Cannae in 216 BC; two Vestals, Opimia and Floronia, were duly convicted: one was entombed, the other committed suicide. Lucius Cantilius, the secretary of the Pontiffs who had deflowered Floronia, was beaten to death. In AD 215 Caracella seduced a Vestal and had her, and two others for good measure, entombed. In AD 220 Elegabalus divorced his wife and married a Vestal, Aquilia Severa, after arranging special dispensation for her to renounce her vows of chastity.

Other extreme measures in AD 83 accompanied Domitian's appointment of himself as perpetual Censor: he censored libellous poetry, banned mime and dancing to eradicate their opportunities for satire, removed an ex-quaestor from the Senate because he was an avid dancer and actor; he also took away the right of disgraced women to travel in litters, to receive legacies and inheritances, and he erased the name of an equestrian from the jurors' lists because he had taken back a wife whom he had previously divorced and accused of adultery.

Adultery was punishable with exile after he revived the Lex Iulia de Adulteriis Coercendis. Homosexual acts with boys of free birth were banned on penalty of death, as was castration, possibly to irritate Titus, who had a predilection for eunuchs "although he was in love with a eunuch named Earinus, he decreed that, from now on, no one in the territory ruled by Rome should be castrated. And so he insulted Titus, who had also been strongly attracted to castrated boys".*

Martial and Statius both 'celebrate' Earinus the eunuch in their poetry: Martial applauds Domitian's legislation against castration, "stolen manhood sliced away by the

---

* Tacitus, *Annals.*

craft of a greedy slavemonger", and the child prostitution which often accompanied it "free to swipe a kid from his mother's breast and set him hawking for filthy money".

Castrated youths could no longer be sold to brothels, while those whose 'operation' predated the law were assigned minimum prices to deter such selling. Martial is quick to illuminate Domitian's hypocrisy in all of this, pointing out that the emperor kept eunuchs in his palace while banning them in the wider empire. To Domitian, Suetonius's "man of excessive lust", sexual intercourse was "bed-wrestling", which gives an idea perhaps of how physical he liked his sex to be.

Domitian was the first to introduce topless female gladiators into the arena, following this with the introduction of female athletes at the games. The women gladiators were pitched against dwarfs to titillate the crowd and satisfy the Romans' fetish for and fascination with combatants with physical deformities. Women afflicted by scoliosis and other disabilities were popular as concubines and populated many a harem. The attraction of male dwarfs lay in their outsized genitalia; Roman *matronae*, apparently, would go and avidly watch when they trained naked. Augustus kept a dwarf called Lucius; Caligula allowed his dwarfs to decide whether their able-bodied colleagues lived or died. Some parents deliberately stunted their children's growth by twisting or breaking their bones—life as a dwarf could be very lucrative. On the downside, however, they were much in demand by magicians, who disembowelled them live, using their intestines in their prognostications.

Some authorities claim that religious minorities, especially Jews and Christians, fared particularly badly under Domitian. *The Book of Revelation*, which mentions at least one martyrdom, is thought by many to have been written during Domitian's reign, based on contemporary events. Eusebius suggests that the social conflict described by *Revelation* reflects Domitian's programme of banishments and executions of Christians. He commanded all David's lineage to be put to death. Notable among the many martyrs who suffered during this persecution was Simeon, Bishop of Jerusalem, who was crucified, and St. John, who was boiled in oil. Flavia, the daughter of a Roman senator, was banished to Pontus; and a law was enacted "that no Christian, once brought before the tribunal, should be exempted from punishment without renouncing his religion".

Reference is often made to the execution of Flavius Clemens, a Roman consul and cousin of the emperor, and to the banishment of his wife, Flavia Domitilla, to the island of Pandateria. Eusebius wrote that Flavia Domitilla was banished because she was a Christian. However, Dio's account reports that she, along with many others, was simply guilty of sympathy for Judaism.

Indeed, many of the many murders Domitian committed seem almost random and even whimsical:

he slew Aelius Lamia for joking remarks, which were reflections on him, it is true, but made long before and harmless; he put to death Salvius Cocceianus, because he had kept the birthday of the emperor Otho, his paternal uncle; Mettius Pompusianus, because it was commonly reported that he had an imperial nativity and carried about a map of the world on parchment and speeches of the kings and generals from Titus Livius, besides giving two of his slaves the names of Mago and Hannibal; Sallustius Lucullus, governor of Britain, for allowing some lances of a new pattern to be named 'Lucullean' after his own name; Junius Rusticus, because he had published eulogies of Paetus Thrasea and Helvidius Priscus and called them the most upright of men.

Perhaps Domitian's most bestial act was when he became determined to rid himself of suspected conspirators. Suspects were subjected to a novel form of eye-watering torture which involved injecting fire into their genitals, and chopping off their hands for good measure. The ignominy suffered by others when they were forced humiliatingly to confess to acts of passive sodomy was paltry by comparison.

ANNIA GALERIA FAUSTINA MINOR (c. AD 130–175) was a daughter of Roman Emperor Antoninus Pius and Roman Empress Faustina the Elder. She was a Roman empress and wife to her maternal cousin Roman Emperor Marcus Aurelius.

Smearing blood had an effect on Faustina, the wife of Marcus Aurelius (r. AD 161–180): she was smitten by a gladiator and finally confessed her passion to her husband. On advice from the Chaldean magi the gladiator in question was executed and Faustina was made to bathe in his blood, and then have sex with her husband still covered in the blood ... all thoughts of the gladiator apparently banished.

Faustina has had a bad press: Cassius Dio and the *Historia Augusta* both accuse Faustina of ordering deaths by poison and execution; she has also been accused of instigating the revolt of Avidius Cassius against her husband; there are reports of serial adultery with sailors, gladiators and senators. The evidence, however, would suggest that Faustina and Aurelius were close and devoted to each other. After her death in an accident at the military camp in Halala (in the Taurus Mountains in Cappadocia), Aurelius was distraught and buried her in the mausoleum of Hadrian in Rome. She was deified: her statue was placed in the Temple of Venus and a temple was dedicated to her in her honour. Halala's name was changed to Faustinopolis and Aurelius opened charity schools for orphan girls called Puellae Faustinianae or 'Girls of Faustina'. The Baths of Faustina in Miletus are named after her.

Commodus (AD 161–192)

"The accession of Commodus marked the descent 'from a kingdom of gold to one of iron and rust'."

Dio 72, 36, 4

Lucius Aurelius Commodus, later Lucius Aelius Aurelius Commodus, reigned as emperor with his father Marcus Aurelius from 177 to his father's death in 180, and then on his own until AD 192. His mother was Aurelius's first cousin, Faustina the Younger, the youngest daughter of Emperor Antoninus Pius. Commodus had an elder twin brother, Titus Aurelius Fulvus Antoninus, who died in 165. In 166, Commodus was made Caesar together with his younger brother, Marcus Annius Verus, but he died in 169 during an operation leaving Commodus as Marcus Aurelius's sole surviving son.

By Roman military standards, the years of Commodus's reign were relatively quiet; this permitted a number of conspiracies to flourish and Commodus to become more and more dictatorial, culminating in the development of a god-like personality cult. This, of course, led to the oppressed senate loathing and fearing him all the more; the army and the people, however, had no such reservations: at first they loved Commodus because of his largesse and because he staged and took part in spectacular and hugely entertaining gladiatorial combats.

AD 182 saw the first conspiracy when a jealous Lucilla acted against her brother along with Tiberius Claudius Pompeianus Quintianus, who was her husband; Tarrutenius Paternus, the head of the Imperial Guard; her daughter Plautia from her first marriage; a nephew of Quintianus also called Quintianus; and her paternal cousins, the former consul Marcus Ummidius Quadratus Annianus and his sister Ummidia Cornificia Faustina (two plotters were her lovers). They tried to murder Commodus as he entered a theatre, but they bungled the job and were seized by the emperor's bodyguard. Quadratus and Quintianus were duly executed while Lucilla was exiled to Capri and later murdered.

Further conspiracies and infighting followed, involving such individuals as Perennis, Cleander, Pompeianus and Pertinax; this served only to drive Commodus out of Rome for longer periods of time, and intensified his megalomania and his delusion that he was a god. Statues sprang up all over the empire portraying Commodus as Hercules, reinforcing the image of him as a demigod, a giant, a protector, and waging a war against beasts and men; he was also the son of Jupiter; he was bringing a new world order to Rome, a Romulus refounding Rome after the devastating fire of 191.

Commodus delegated many of the affairs of state to one of his prefects, Perennis, so that he could focus on his degenerate lifestyle; according to the *Historia Augusta*:

Above: Commodus. (Kunsthistorisches Museum, Vienna/ AuCristianChirita)

Right: Statue of Venus emerging from her bath; the face depicts Annia Lucilla. (Dresden Albertinum/ JoJan, modifications par QuartierLatin1968)

"Even from his earliest years he was base and dishonourable, and cruel and lewd, defiled of mouth, moreover, and debauched." He was in the habit of visiting brothels and taverns at night. Evidently, he ran a harem of 300 girls and women and 300 boys, some of whom had been kidnapped.

He raped his other sisters, had an affair with a cousin of his father's, and named one of his concubines after his mother. When he caught his wife in the act of adultery, he banished her, and later put her to death. His concubines were raped in front of him; he was, again according to Suetonius, "not free from the disgrace of intimacy with young men, defiling every part of his body in dealings with persons of either sex". Among his retainers were men whom he rechristened after the genitals of both sexes and whom he would kiss in public; one of these was a man with a penis larger than that of most large animals, whom he called Onos because he was hung like a donkey. He treated Onos with great affection, made him rich and appointed him to the priesthood of the Rural Hercule.

As with previous emperors, his cruelty seems arbitrary, casual and whimsical; the *Historia Augusta* gives us this incredible account of Commodus' reign of terror: "Even as a child he was gluttonous and lewd. While a youth, he disgraced every class of men in his company and was disgraced in turn by them. Whosoever ridiculed him he cast to the wild beasts. And one man, who had merely read the book by Tranquillus containing the life of Caligula, he ordered cast to the wild beasts, because Caligula and he had the same birthday." His sense of humour too, was destructive. For example, "he put a starling on the head of one man who, as he noticed, had a few white hairs, resembling worms, among the black, and caused his head to fester through the continual pecking of the bird's beak—the bird, of course, imagining that it was pursuing worms. One corpulent person he cut open down the middle of his belly, so that his intestines gushed forth. Other men he dubbed one-eyed or one-footed, after he himself had plucked out one of their eyes or cut off one of their feet. He kept among his minions certain men named after the genitalia of both sexes, and on these he liked to bestow kisses. It is claimed that he often mixed human excrement with the most expensive foods, and he did not refrain from tasting them, mocking the rest of the company, as he thought. He displayed two misshapen hunchbacks on a silver platter after smearing them with mustard, and then straightway advanced and enriched them ... He used to bathe seven and eight times a day, and was in the habit of eating while in the baths. He would enter the temples of the gods defiled with adulteries and human blood. He even aped a surgeon, going so far as to bleed men to death with scalpels."

He renamed Rome Colonia Lucia Annia Commodiana and the months of the year after his twelve names: Lucius, Aelius, Aurelius, Commodus, Augustus, Herculeus, Romanus, Exsuperatorius, Amazonius, Invictus, Felix, and Pius. The legions were renamed Commodianae, the fleet became Alexandria Commodiana Togata, the Senate the Commodian Fortunate Senate, his palace and the Roman people themselves were all given the name Commodianus, and the day on which these reforms were decreed was to be called Dies Commodianus.

Commodus then saw himself as the embodiment of Rome and of all things Roman. He had the head of the Colossus of Nero next to the Colosseum replaced with his own head, armed it with a club and placed a bronze lion at its feet to make it look like Hercules Romanus.

In November 192, Commodus staged his Plebeian Games, in which he shot hundreds of animals with arrows and javelins every morning, and himself fought as a gladiator every afternoon, winning every fight. He was fiercely proud of his left-handedness: he added an inscription on the Hercules statue boasting of being, according to Dio, "the only left-handed fighter to conquer twelve times one thousand men". He was a skilled archer, who would shoot the heads off ostriches at full pelt, and kill a panther as it attacked a victim in the arena.

His antics in the arena repelled many Romans, prompting rumours that he was actually the son, not of Marcus Aurelius, but of a gladiator whom his mother Faustina had taken as a lover at the seaside town of Caieta. Of course, Commodus always won his battles in the arena. Privately, he used to slaughter his sparring partners. For every appearance, he charged the city of Rome a million sesterces, putting massive strain on the Roman treasury. Often, wounded soldiers and amputees would be sent into the arena for Commodus to slay with his sword in the style of Hercules; or they would be tethered together for Commodus to club to death, pretending they were giants.

In the arena, exotic animals were no safer. Commodus once killed a hundred lions in a single day. Later, he decapitated a running ostrich with a specially designed dart and afterwards carried his sword and the bleeding head of the dead bird over to the section where the senators sat, motioning as though they were next. On another occasion, Commodus killed three elephants single-handedly.

It took very little to incur Commodus's wrath, and the sharp end of his sword; just making him angry was sometimes enough: he whimsically attempted to exterminate the house of the Quinctilii when Condianus and Maximus were executed, on the pretext that, while they were not implicated in any plots, their wealth and talent would make them unhappy with the way things were.

But Romans had had enough. By 192 Rome and the Senate had had its fill of Commodus's corruption, his Herculean impersonations and his demeaning obsession with the world of the gladiator with his many public displays in the arena. A conspiracy was formed comprising his inner cabinet: his mistress Marcia, his chamberlain Eclectus, and the praetorian prefect Quintus Aemilius Laetus; the aim was to remove Commodus and replace him with Pertinax. Marcia poisoned his beef but Commodus vomited up the poisoned meal; undeterred the conspirators summoned his wrestling partner Narcissus to strangle him in his bath. Commodus died and the Senate declared him a public enemy and issued a de facto *damnatio memoriae*. They restored the original name to the city of Rome as well as all the institutions to their original names.

Dio, a contemporary, tries to analyze and explain the character of Commodus: "[Commodus was] not naturally wicked but, on the contrary, was as guileless as any man that ever lived. His great simplicity, however, together with his cowardice, made him the slave of his companions, and it was through them that he at first, out of ignorance, missed the better life and then was led on into lustful and cruel habits, which soon became second nature.

Historia Augusta has the last word: "Let the memory of the murderer and the gladiator be utterly wiped away. Let the statues of the murderer and the gladiator be toppled. Let the memory of the foul gladiator be utterly extinguished. Throw the gladiator into the charnel-house. Listen, Caesar: let the slayer be dragged with the hook. In the manner of our fathers let the slayer of the Senate be dragged with the hook. More savage than Domitian, more foul than Nero. As he did unto others, let it be done unto him."

LUCIUS AURELIUS VERUS (AD 130–169) was the co-emperor of Rome with his adoptive brother Marcus Aurelius from 161 until his own death in 169. Hadrian had adopted the father of Lucius Verus, Lucius Aelius Caesar, with a view to him succeeding as emperor of Rome. Lucius Verus himself was adopted by Antoninus Pius in AD 138 and ruled jointly with Marcus Aurelius from 161 to 169. *Historia Augusta* is our only extensive source for his life, and it is from this that he quickly won a reputation not only for "the licence of an unbridled life, but also by adulteries and by love-affairs with young men.

He allegedly set up a cook shop [notorious haunts of prostitutes] in his home, where he held banquets and had all manner of foul persons serve him ... and that he so rivalled Caligula, Nero, and Vitellius in their vices as to wander about at night through taverns and brothels with only a common travelling-cap for a head-covering, revel with various rowdies, and engage in brawls, concealing his identity the while; and often, they say, when he returned, his face was beaten black and blue. Rumour had it that he had a relationship with his mother-in-law, Faustina and that she murdered him by having poison sprinkled on his oysters, because he had revealed the affair to her daughter".

Lucius Verus (AD 130–169). (National Archaeological Museum of Athens/ Dantadd)

THE PERSECUTION IN LYON in AD 177 was a coordinated persecution of Christians in Lugdunum, (present-day Lyon), during the reign of Marcus Aurelius (r. 161–180). Our only source is a letter preserved in Eusebius's *Ecclesiastical History* 5, 1.

The first recorded Christian community established in Lugdunum was in the 2nd century led by a bishop named Pothinus from Asia Minor. As far as Roman governors were concerned, being a Christian was in itself a subversive act, because it was a refusal to sacrifice to the gods of Rome, including the deified emperor.

By 177, many of the Christians around Vienne and Lyons were Greeks from Asia. Before the actual outbreak of violence, Christians were forbidden to enter the marketplace, the forum, the baths, or to appear in any public places. If they did appear in public they were subject to derision and mockery, beaten, and robbed by mobs. The homes of Christians were vandalized. The martyrs of Lyons were accused of "Thyestean banquets and Oedipean intercourse"—cannabalism and incest.

The authorities—the chiliarch, a military commander, and the duumvir, a civil magistrate—arrested Christians and interrogated them in public in the forum. They were then imprisoned until the governor returned. Eusebius tells us that the presbyter, or elder, St. Irenaeus was sent with a letter from members of the Church of Lyons now awaiting martyrdom, to Eleutherus, Bishop of Rome.

When the governor got back to Lugdunum, he repeated the public interrogation, abusing the Christians so badly that Vettius Epagathus, a Christian and man of high social standing, requested permission to testify on behalf of the accused. This was refused and instead the governor arrested Vettius Epagathus when he confessed to being a Christian.

The Christians were tortured while the authorities continued to apprehend others. Two of their pagan servants were seized and, fearing torture, falsely charged the Christians with incest and cannibalism. In the end, all forty-eight were killed, some of whom had recanted but later returned to the faith. The elderly Bishop Pothinus, first Bishop of Lugdunum, was beaten and whipped, and died soon after in prison.

A slave, Blandina, was subjected to the cruellest of torture. The legate received instructions from Marcus Aurelius allowing the Roman citizens who persisted in the faith to be executed by beheading, but those without citizenship were to be tortured. Even the executioners were exhausted "as they did not know what more they could do to her". She remained obdurate and repeated to every question, "I am a Christian, and we commit no wrongdoing." Blandina was then subjected to new tortures with a number of companions in the town's amphitheatre. She was stripped and hung on a stake as fodder for the beasts which had been let loose on her. When none of the beasts touched her she was brought back to the prison. In a bid to persuade her to recant, she was led into the arena to witness the sufferings of her companions. Finally, as the last of the martyrs, she was whipped, placed on a red-hot grate, enclosed in a net and thrown before a wild bull which tossed her into the air on his horns. In the end, she was killed off with a dagger.

Septimius Severus (AD 145–211)

Lucius Septimius Severus Augustus was Roman emperor from AD 193 to 211. He and the Senate had a fractious relationship: the Senate was always uncomfortable with the fact that Severus had acceded to the throne through a military coup. Severus responded by ordering the execution of many senators on charges of corruption or conspiracy, replacing them with people he could trust.

Christians too suffered. Eusebius called Severus a persecutor while Tertullian records that Severus was pro-Christian, to the extent that his physician was a Christian. Nevertheless, his reign saw numerous persecutions including those known in the Roman Martyrology: the martyrs of Madaura, Charalambos and Perpetua and Felicity in Africa.

The martyrdom in 202 of Bishop Charalambos of Magnesia in Assyria was the emperor's *pièce de résistance*; at the time Charalambos was reputedly 113 years old. When the Proconsul Lucian and the military governor Lucius got wind of his preaching the saint was arrested and tried, where he confessed his faith in Christ. He was then cruelly tortured: his aged body was lacerated with iron hooks, and the skin was scraped from his body. Brave and resilient beyond belief, Charalambos wittily said to his torturers, "Thank you, my brethren, for scraping off the old body and renewing my soul for new and eternal life."

The atrocity had an immediate effect on those who witnessed it: two soldiers, Porphyrius and Baptus, were so shocked that they, according to the hagiography, confessed their faith in Christ, for which they were instantly beheaded. Three women who were watching the torture began to glorify Christ, and were also quickly martyred for their troubles. Lucius was incandescent and began to torture Charalambos himself—but all of a sudden his forearms were sliced off as if by a sword. The governor Lucian

Above :Tondo showing the Severan dynasty, the family of Septimius Severus c. 199: Severus, Julia Domna, Caracalla and Geta (erased). (Antikensammlung, Berlin/ PD-Art)

Right: Septimius Severus. (Ny Carlsberg Glyptotek, Copenhagen/ Carole Raddato)

then spat in the face of the saint, and immediately Lucian's head was swivelled about so that he faced backwards. Lucian and Lucius both prayed for mercy, were healed by the saint, and became Christians.

Enter Septimius Severus who personally prolonged the torture. Condemned to death and led to the place of execution, Charalambos prayed that God grant the place where his relics were to repose might never suffer famine or disease. The saint then gave up his soul to God even before the executioner had struck his neck. Severus's daughter Gallina was so upset by his death that she was converted and buried Charalambos herself.

The fate of Perpetua and Felicity is featured in *The Passion of Saint Perpetua, Saint Felicitas, and their Companions*—one of the oldest and most famous early Christian texts. It survives in both Latin and Greek forms, and is believed to be the actual prison diary of the young mother and martyr Perpetua.

The Passion records that a slave named Revocatus, his fellow slave Felicitas, two freemen Saturninus and Secundulus, and Perpetua, who were all catechumens (Christians being instructed in the faith but not yet baptized), were arrested and executed at the military games in celebration of Septimus Severus's birthday. A man named Saturus who voluntarily went before the magistrate and proclaimed himself

The 20,000 martyrs of Nicomedia. (http://days.pravoslavie.ru/Images/ii6938&3911.htm)

a Christian suffered the same fate. *Historia Augusta* has it that Perpetua, Felicity and the others were martyred according to a decree of Severus outlawing conversions to Judaism and Christianity.

Perpetua's diary opens with her and her father at loggerheads: he wants her to recant her faith but Perpetua refuses, and soon after is baptized before being imprisoned. Bribing the guards permits her to move to a better part of the prison, where she nurses her baby who is allowed to stay in prison with her for the time being. On the day of the games, the martyrs are led into the amphitheatre where the baying crowd demands that they be scourged before a line of gladiators; then a boar, a bear, and a leopard are set on the men, and a wild cow on the women. Wounded by the beasts, they give each other the kiss of peace and are then put to the sword. Perpetua's death is described as follows: "But Perpetua, that she might have some taste of pain, was pierced between the bones and shrieked out; and when the swordsman's hand wandered still (for he was a novice), herself set it upon her own neck. Perchance so great a woman could not else have been slain (being feared of the unclean spirit) had she not herself so willed it."

Caracalla (AD 188–217)

"His way of life was evil and he was more brutal even than his cruel father. He was a glutton and addicted to wine, hated by his household and detested in every camp

86

save that of the praetorian guard; and between him and his brother there was no resemblance whatever."

Historia Augusta 9, 3

Caracalla, Marcus Aurelius Severus Antoninus Augustus, ruled from 198 to 211 with his father, Septimius Severus, until his death in Eboracum, modern York. The notoriously unreliable *Historia Augusta* tells us that he was a sensitive boy but when he passed beyond the age of a boy, either by his father's advice or through a natural cunning, or because he thought that he must imitate Alexander of Macedonia, he became more reserved and stern and even somewhat savage in expression, and indeed so much so that many were unable to believe that he was the same person whom they had known as a boy.

His joint rule with his brother Publius Septimius Antoninus Geta from 209 was a disaster and culminated in the murder of Geta, of his former cousin and wife Fulvia

Caracalla is behind the seated Emperor Septimius Severus with Julia Domna next to him and Geta between his two sisters. The occasion is the gala given by Severus in AD 203 when he bestowed on Caracalla the title of Antoninus Caesar in the Colosseum. By Lawrence Alma-Tadema (1836–1912) in 1907.

Plautilla (whom he despised) by strangulation after exile on Lipari, of his daughter and other members of the family of his former father-in-law Gaius Fulvius Plautianus, commander of the Praetorian Guard, who himself was executed for treason. Caracalla then issued a *damnatio memoriae* against his brother's memory: Geta's image was erased from all paintings, coins were melted down, statues were destroyed, his name was struck from papyrus records, and it became a capital offence to speak or write Geta's name. In all an estimated 20,000 people were then butchered, mainly Geta's guards and advisers, friends, and military staff: here is the description in *Historia Augusta*: "The following day he proceeded to the Capitol; here he spoke cordially to those whom he was planning to put to death and then went back to the Palace leaning on the arm of Papinian and of Cilo. Here he saw Geta's mother and some other women weeping for his brother's death, and he decided to kill them; but he was deterred by thinking how this would merely add to the cruelty of having slain his brother. Laetus, however, he forced to commit suicide, sending him the poison himself; he had been the first to counsel the death of Geta and was himself the first to be killed."

Historia Augusta again: "Afterwards, however, the emperor frequently bewailed his death. Many others, too, who had been privy to Geta's murder were put to death, and likewise a man who paid honours to his portrait ... After this he gave orders that his cousin Afer should be killed, although on the previous day he had sent him a portion of food from his own table. Afer in fear of the assassins threw himself from a window and crawled away to his wife with a broken leg, but he was none the less seized by the murderers, who ridiculed him and put him to death. Pompeianus too was killed, the grandson of the Emperor Marcus ... he was killed in such a way as to seem to have been murdered by robbers. Next, in the emperor's own presence, Papinian was struck with an axe by some soldiers and so slain ... Patruinus, too, was slain by his order, and that in front of the Temple of the Deified Pius, and his body as well as Papinian's were dragged about through the streets without any regard for decency. Also Papinian's son was killed, who, as a quaestor and only three days before, had given a lavish spectacle ... Then there was a slaughtering in all manner of places. Even in the public baths there was slaughter, and some too were killed while dining, among them Sammonicus Serenus, many of whose books dealing with learned subjects are still in circulation. Cilo, moreover, twice prefect and consul, incurred the utmost danger merely because he had counselled harmony between the brothers. For not until after the city-soldiers had seized Cilo, tearing off his senator's robe and pulling off his boots, did Caracalla check their violence."

Caracalla became obsessed with Alexander the Great, mimicking him and copying his tactics. While planning his invasion of the Parthia, Caracalla deployed 16,000 of his men in Macedonian-style phalanxes, despite the fact that in the Roman army the phalanx was an obsolete tactical formation. Caracalla's obsession took him to

Caracalla from a marble statue
reworked as a bust in AD 212.
(Naples National Archaeological,
from the baths of Caracalla/
Marie-Lan Nguyen)

Alexandria where he persecuted philosophers of the Aristotelian school on the basis
that Aristotle had supposedly poisoned Alexander.

Worse followed: his assaults on the German tribes in 212/13 were accompanied by
his pointless butchering of an allied German force. When the Alexandrians heard
Caracalla's claims that he had killed his brother Geta in self-defence, they produced
a satire mocking this as well as Caracalla's other fantasies. In 215 Caracalla travelled
to Alexandria and responded to the insult by slaughtering the deputation of leading
citizens who had unsuspectingly assembled to greet him; he then unleashed his troops
on Alexandria for several days of unbridled looting and plunder. In Dacia he murdered
thousands during his campaign against the Lucanians: "men were condemned to death
for having urinated in places where there were statues or busts of the emperor or for
having removed garlands from his busts." *Historia Augusta* gives us the unlikely story
of Caracalla's incest and subsequent marriage to his mother, Julia Domna: "She was
by repute a very beautiful woman, and one day she carelessly showed 'a considerable part of her person' in Caracalla's presence. Caracalla responded, 'I should like to,
if I might,' whereupon Julia replied, 'If you wish, you may; are you not aware that you

Dedicated in AD 212, the baths of Caracalla could hold 1,600 bathers. The emperor can be seen entering in the background. Shelley wrote Prometheus Unbound in the ruins here. By Lawrence Alma-Tadema (1836–1912) in 1899.

are the emperor and that you make the laws and do not receive them?' They had sex and Caracalla contracted a marriage, 'and to fratricide he added incest, for he joined to himself in marriage the woman whose son he had recently slain'."

MACRINUS (Marcus Opellius Severus Macrinus Augustus) (c. AD 165–218) was emperor from April 217 to June 218. He reigned jointly with his young son Diadumenianus; he was an equestrian and was the first emperor not to have come from the senatorial class. Macrinus served under Caracalla as a praetorian prefect and looked after Rome's civil affairs. He later conspired against Caracalla and had him murdered in a bid to protect his own life, after a prophecy that he would depose and succeed the emperor.

In 217, Julia Maesa, Elagabalus's grandmother, put it about that Elagabalus was the illegitimate son of Caracalla. On 16 May, Elagabalus was proclaimed emperor by the Legio III Gallica at Raphanea, Macrinus then travelled to Apamea and conferred the title of Augustus onto his son, Diadumenianus, and made him co-emperor. Diadumenianus was sent into the care of Artbanus V of Parthia but was captured at Zeugma and killed in June 218. Diadumenianus's reign lasted a total of fourteen months; he was about ten years old when he died. Macrinus, on learning of his son's death, tried to escape captivity, but he injured himself and was afterward executed in Cappadocia; his head was sent to Elagabalus. Diadumenianus's head was also cut off and sent to Elagabalus as a trophy. Just how unpopular Macrinus was in Rome is reflected in the *damnatio memoriae* issued on him and on his son.

Macrinus. (Capitoline Museum/ José Luiz Bernardes Ribeiro)

Historia Augusta would have it that Macrinus was "arrogant and bloodthirsty and desirous of ruling in military fashion ... he even crucified soldiers and always used the punishments meted out to slaves, and when he had to deal with a mutiny among the troops, he usually decimated the soldiers, but sometimes he only cen-timated them ... It would be too long to relate all his acts of brutality, but never-theless one [is described here], no great one in his belief, yet one which was more distressing than all his tyrannical cruelties. There were some soldiers who had had intercourse with their host's maid-servant, who for some time had led a life of ill-repute. Learning of their offence through one of his spies, he ordered them to be brought before him and questioned them as to whether it were really true. When their guilt was proved, he gave orders that two oxen of extraordinary size should be cut open rapidly while still alive, and that the soldiers should be thrust one into each, with their heads protruding so that they could talk to each other. In this way he inflicted punishment on them, though neither our ancestors nor the men of his own time ever ordained any such penalty, even for those guilty of adultery ... A tribune who allowed a sentry-post to be left unguarded he caused to be bound under a wheeled waggon and then dragged living or dead all through the entire march. He even reproduced the punishment inflicted by Mezentius, who used to bind live men to dead and thus force them to die consumed by slow decay." He also put living men into walls, which he then built up. Those guilty of adultery he always burned alive, fastening their bodies together.

Elagabalus (c. AD 203–222)

"An unspeakably disgusting life."

Niebuhr, *History of Rome* 144

His real name was Marcus Aurelius Antoninus Augustus but he is usually known as Elagabalus or Heliogabalus, and was emperor from 218 to 222. Elagabalus was Syrian, the second son of Julia Soaemias and Sextus Varius Marcellus. The name Elagabalus comes from the god Elagabal for whom the young Elegabal served as a priest in his mother's hometown of Emesa (modern-day Homs in Syria). Only after his death was he called Elagabalus.

Elagabalus became emperor at the age of fourteen, in the wake of some adept scheming on the part of his grandmother (and Caracalla's maternal aunt), Julia Maesa, in AD 217. That year, the reigning emperor, the dissolute Caracalla, was assassinated and replaced by his Praetorian Prefect, Marcus Opellius Macrinus. Julia Maesa,

Right: Elagabalus. (Palazzo Nuovo, Musei Capitolini, Rome/ José Luiz Bernardes Ribeiro)

Below: The roses of Heliogabalus by Lawrence Alma-Tadema in 1888.

in exile, wasted no time in stoking a rebellion among the III Gallica legion to have Elagabalus declared emperor on 8 June 218, at the battle of Antioch. The pretext was that Elagabalus was the illegitimate son of Caracalla.

Elagabalus began his reign as he intended to go on, with a total disregard for Roman religious convention and sexual taboos. He had a short life, but a consistently active sex life; he was a notorious deviant, beset by gender confusion and depravity. He was married at least five times, he showed favour to his many male lovers and prostituted himself around the imperial palace. For example, Elagabalus tried to have one lover, the charioteer Hierocles, declared Caesar, while the athlete Aurelius Zoticus was appointed to the influential, and convenient, position of Master of the Chamber, or Cubicularius. To Elagabalus, Hierocles was his husband, reputedly declaring, "[I am] delighted to be called the mistress, the wife, the Queen of Hierocles" Had Hierocles succeeded in becoming Caesar he would have been successor to the imperial throne. However, Hierocles was executed, along with other members of the court, when the emperor was deposed in AD 222. Apparently he was anally abused with a sword.

Before all that, though, it was not long before Elagabalus started to alienate the Praetorian Guard, the Senate, and his subjects. At first, the unpredictable and volatile emperor got on tolerably well with Julia Maesa and Julia Soaemias, his mother. He allowed them access to the Senate, the first women to be (officially) permitted there; they were honoured with senatorial titles: Soaemias became Clarissima, and *Maesa Mater Castrorum et Senatus* ('Mother of the Army Camp and of the Senate').

Other women fared less well. Even the Vestal Virgins were not safe; he married the Vestal Virgin Aquilia Severa, in a bid to produce "divine children". A more shocking and flagrant breach of Roman religious law and convention could not be imagined. It was the ultimate in hubris and impiety, in treason even. The traditional punishment for a Vestal who misplaced her virginity was the agonizingly slow death by live entombment. Religious symbolism may have led Elagabalus to marry Severa; Elagabalus was an adherent to the eastern sun-god El-Gabal and, by marrying Severa, he was forging a union between the sun-god and Vesta. The 'marriage' was soon annulled and Elagabalus wed Annia Faustina, a less controversial bride. The extremely wealthy Faustina had recently been widowed when her late husband, Pomponius Bassus, was executed for subversion and treason. Faustina did not last long and was divorced so that her short-lived imperial husband could return to the lapsed Vestal Virgin, claiming that the original divorce was invalid.

Elagabalus naturally wanted to become the high priest of his new religion; to achieve this he had himself circumcised. More sacrilege and iconoclasm followed

An 18th-century mural of Elagabalus at castle Forchtenstein Burgenland in Austria. (Glst2media)

when he removed some of the most sacred and revered relics of traditional Roman religion to the Elagabalium, including the symbol of the Great Mother, the fire of Vesta, the Shields of the Salii and the Palladium; no other god could now be worshipped without Elagabal.

Elagabalus's first wife was the noblewoman Julia Cornelia Paula, Empress of Rome from 219–220, then divorced so that her husband could marry the Vestal Virgin. His affairs with Hierocles and Aurelius Zoticus, however, seemed to have been pursued with much greater enthusiasm than any of his heterosexual marriages. Indeed, according to *Historia Augusta*, Elagabalus actually married Zoticus at a lavish ceremony in Rome. By now he was now routinely applying eye makeup, depilating body hair and wearing wigs before prostituting himself in taverns, brothels and even in the imperial palace. Dio gives the sordid details: "Finally, he set aside a room in the palace and there committed his indecencies, always standing nude at the door of the room, as the harlots do, and shaking the curtain which hung from gold rings, while in a soft and melting voice he solicited the passersby. There were, of course, men who had been specially instructed to play their part. For, as in other matters, so in this business, too, he had numerous agents who sought out those who could best please him by their foulness. He would collect money from his patrons and give himself airs over his gains; he would also dispute with his associates in this shameful occupation, claiming that he had more lovers than they and took in more money."

The *Historia Augusta*, if it is to believed, gives us a startling insight into the emperor's perverted sense of humour: "The recipient of lust in every orifice of his body, he sent agents looking for men with large penises to satisfy his passions. He put a dancer-cum-actor, Cordius, in charge of the Praetorian Guard, and a barber, Claudius, of the grain supply. The size of a man's organ often determined the post he was given. He would often lock his friends up when they were drunk and suddenly, in the night, let in lions and leopards and bears—previously rendered harmless—so that when they woke up they would find at dawn, or what is worse, at night, lions, bears and panthers in the same bedroom as themselves. Several of them died as a result of this."

He opened the bath of Plautinus to the public in order to attract men with unusually large penises. He scoured the whole city searching for *onobeli*, those who were inordinately well endowed, hung like a donkey. Mythology even could not escape his indecency, *Historia Augusta* again: "He used to have the story of Paris played in his house, and he himself would take the rôle of Venus, and suddenly drop his clothes to the ground and fall naked on his knees, one hand on his breast, the other on his genitals, his buttocks projecting meanwhile and thrust back in front of his partner in depravity."

Things went a step further when he offered huge amounts of money to any physician who could give him permanent female genitalia or, in the words of Dio, "to contrive a woman's vagina in his body by means of an incision". Dio also alludes to castration when he tells us that a physician was asked to employ his skill to make him bisexual by means of an anterior incision. He seems even to have been partial to child sacrifice, collecting "children of noble birth and beautiful appearance", and employing magicians to perform daily sacrifices so that he could examine the children's internal organs and torture the victims.

Credit where it is due, though. The emperor obviously saw what was coming to him in his short and egregious life; Dio says he had a suicide tower built "with gilded and jewelled boards spread underneath in front of him … saying that 'even his death ought to be costly and of an extravagant pattern'".

On 11 March AD 222 Elagabalus and his mother, Julia Soaemias, were butchered by the Praetorian Guard. Dio takes up the lurid story: "So he made an attempt to flee, and would have got away somewhere by being placed in a chest, had he not been discovered and slain, at the age of eighteen. His mother, who embraced him and clung tightly to him, perished with him; their heads were cut off and their bodies, after being stripped naked, were first dragged all over the city; [an attempt to shove them into a sewer was thwarted because the opening was not wide enough]; then the mother's body was cast aside somewhere or other while his was thrown into the [Tiber]."

Many of Elagabalus's friends and colleagues were then murdered, including Hierocles. His sacrileges were reversed. Women were again barred from the Senate and *damnatio memoriae was* applied. Gibbon was no fan, and indignantly highlights just one of many instances of the emperor's decadence; the effeminate wearing of silks: "Two hundred years after the age of Pliny, the use of pure, or even of mixed silks, was confined to the female sex, till the opulent citizens of Rome and the provinces were insensibly familiarized with the example of Elagabalus, the first who, by this effeminate habit, had sullied the dignity of an emperor and a man."[*]

Despite the *damnatio*, many works of art and literature have been spawned by the emperor's memory down the years. He lives on in the Spanish word *heliogábalo*, which means 'a person subsumed by gluttony'.

---

[*] Gibbon, *The History of the Decline and Fall of the Roman Empire*, see also chapter 6: "[Elagabalus] abandoned himself to the grossest pleasures and ungoverned fury."

SEVERUS ALEXANDER (AD 207–235) would succeed his cousin Elagabalus. He reigned from AD 222 to 235. Severus represents, in many ways, the opposite to the monsters described in these pages, reversing and nullifying much of Elagabalus's sordid and deprived behaviour. As a thirteen-year-old emperor it is hardly surprising that he was dominated by his grandmother, Julia Maesa, and his mother, Julia Avita Mamaea. Julia Mamaea was a virtuous woman, scandal-free and devoted to the education of her son. Alexander married three times, most famously to the sixteen-year-old Sallustia Orbiana whom he married in AD 225, a union arranged by Alexander's mother. However, when Orbiana received the title of Augusta, Mamaea became increasingly jealous and resentful. Alexander divorced and exiled her in 227. The second wife was Sulpicia Memmia, from one of the most ancient patrician families in Rome. Alexander fathered no children with any of his three wives.

In complete contrast to Elagabalus, Alexander dismissed all eunuchs from his service and commanded that they should serve his wife as slaves, reducing their number and removing them from all duties in the palace except the care of the women's baths. He used to say that eunuchs were the third sex of the human race, one not to be seen or employed by men and scarcely even by women of noble birth. When one of them sold a false promise in his name he ordered him to be crucified along a busy road frequented by slaves.

In his efforts to reverse some of the debauchery established by his cousin, he forbade mixed bathing, previously outlawed before being permitted by Elagabalus. He imposed taxes on procurers, whores and catamites and used the revenues to restore the theatre, the Circus, the Amphitheatre and the Stadium. He wanted to ban catamites altogether but desisted in case it simply drove the practice underground. He banned women of dubious reputation from attending the levees of his mother and his wife.

All dwarfs, both male and female, idiots, catamites who had good voices, every kind of entertainer at table, and actors of pantomimes

Obverse of a denarius of Severus Alexander. (York Museums Trust)

were made public property; those, however, who were useless were assigned, each to different towns for support, so that no one town might be burdened by too many beggars. The eunuchs were given to his friends, with the proviso that if they did not return to honest ways, it would be lawful to put them to death without authority from the courts. Women of ill repute, of whom he arrested an enormous number, he ordered to become public prostitutes. He later deported all catamites, some of whom were conveniently drowned by shipwreck in transit.

Alexander also tried hard to reduce the luxuries that had stifled Rome for centuries. He sold all his jewels with the proceeds going to the public treasury, saying that men had no need of trinkets, and that the women of the royal household should be content with one hairnet, a pair of earrings, a necklace of pearls, a diadem to wear while sacrificing, a single cloak ornamented with gold, and one robe with an embroidered border, not to contain more than six ounces of gold. He set a fine example for good men to follow while his wife was an exemplar for *matronae*.

Dexippus of Athens tells us that Alexander married the daughter of Macrinus and that he gave this man the name of Caesar. However, when Macrinus tried to kill him Alexander not only put Macrinus to death but also divorced his wife.*

There is an interesting footnote to Alexander's story. Alsawad, king of one of Alexander's client states was under siege by Ataxerxes the Persian emperor; Artaxerxes knew of Alsawad's daughter and proposed a marriage alliance. Alsawad rejected this but the daughter liked the idea of being a Persian princess and sent letters to Artaxerxes by an early version of airmail, on arrows. The Persian got back to her with a request that she disclose where their weakest defences were so that he could break in with his army and marry her. This she did, the Persians took the city and Alsawad's daughter married Artaxerxes. After a while the Persian decided to test the girl and asked her how her father had treated her; she responded that he was totally devoted to her and was in fact the perfect father. At this Artaxerxes told her she was not worthy of life and that, if she had betrayed a father who had been so good to her, what could he expect in the way of fidelity. He then ordered her to be tied by her hair to a wild horse's tail; the horse galloped off and she was torn to pieces.

---

* P. Herennius Dexippus of Athens. His *Chronicle*, frequently cited in the later biographies of *Historia Augusta*, begins with the mythical period and extends down to AD 268. He held important municipal offices in Athens, and about 267 AD, with the aid of a hastily collected army, he repelled an invasion of the Goths (the Heruli).

TRAJAN DECIUS (Caesar Gaius Messius Quintus Trajanus Decius Augustus c. 201–251) was emperor from 249 to 251. When in 250 Decius issued a decree requiring public sacrifice to the Roman gods in a form of a testimonial of allegiance to the emperor, an unintended consequence was a de facto persecution of the Christians. Christians were never singled out specifically, indeed no religions were and Jews were even exempted, but inevitably Christians were among those caught in the net of the roving commissions which visited the cities, towns and villages to supervise the sacrifices and to issue written certificates (*libelli*) to all citizens who carried them out. Refusal to comply was punished by arrest, imprisonment, torture and execution. Christians, therefore, apostatized or fled to safe havens in the countryside. Amongst them was Cyprian, bishop of Carthage; others bought their certif-

A Byzantine fresco, from Ohrid, Macedonia dated 1295, of Saint Mercurius, a Christian victim of the Decian persecution.

icates on the black market. Those that refused and were killed as a result included Pope Fabian, Babylas of Antioch and Alexander of Jerusalem.

Here is an example of a *libellus* discovered in Egypt: "To those in charge of the sacrifices of the village Theadelphia, from Aurelia Bellias, daughter of Peteres, and her daughter Kapinis. We have always been constant in sacrificing to the gods, and now too, in your presence, in accordance with the regulations, I have poured libations and sacrificed and tasted the offerings, and I ask you to certify this for us below. May you continue to prosper. [Second person's handwriting.] We, Aurelius Serenus and Aurelius Hermas, saw you sacrificing. [Third person's handwriting.] I, Hermas, certify. The first year of the Emperor Caesar Gaius Messias Quintus Traianus Decius Pius Felix Augustus, Pauni 27."

Intended or not, this was the first time that Christians in the Empire had been forced by imperial edict to choose between their religion and their lives. For many, such monstrous tyranny was unheard of until the edict of Decius.

Valerian (c. AD 193–264)

Valerian (Publius Licinius Valerianus Augustus) was Roman emperor from AD 253 to 260. He took the imperial persecution of Christians to another level when, during his wars with the Persians, he sent two letters to the Senate demanding a more robust policy be taken against Christians. The first, in 257 was a repeat of Decius's edict, ordering Christian clergy to perform sacrifices to the Roman gods or face banishment. The second, in 258, ordered the execution of Christian leaders. It also required Christian senators and *equites* to worship the Roman gods or lose their status and property, and face execution if they refused. Roman *matronae* who did not apostatize would lose their property and be exiled; government officials and members of the imperial household who refused to worship the Roman gods were to be reduced to slavery and sent to work on the imperial estates.

Prominent executions included Saint Prudent at Narbonne in 257. The next year Pope Sixtus II, Saint Romanus Ostiarius, Saint Lawrence, Saints Denis in Paris, Pontius in Cimiez, Cyprian in Carthage and Eugenia in Rome were all executed; in 259 Saint Patroclus was executed at Troyes and Saint Fructuosus at Tarragona. (Valerian's son Gallienus became emperor in 260, and would rescind the decree.)

A bas relief of Emperor Valerian standing at the background and held captive by Shapur I found at Naqsh-e Rustam, Shiraz, Iran. The kneeling man is probably Philip the Arab. (Sahand Ace)

In 260 Valerian's army was defeated by the Sassanian Persian despot Shapur I at the disastrous battle of Edessa; Valerian negotiated a peace settlement but Shapur reneged on this and held Valerian and his wife, Egnatia Mariniana, prisoner. Valerian, according to Eutropius, "grew old in ignominious slavery among the Parthians". The anti-Persian Christian Lactantius maintains that Valerian was subjected to the greatest humiliation by his captors and was used as a human footstool by Shapur when mounting his horse. Shapur also allowed anyone who wanted to sodomize Valerian to do so, and had dogs bugger him as well; Egnatia Mariniana suffered the same atrocity.

Valerian could only take so much and offered Shapur a huge ransom for his release. In response, Shapur forced Valerian to swallow molten gold; another version says that Valerian was killed by being flayed alive. Whatever, Shapur then had Valerian skinned and stuffed with straw and preserved as a trophy in the Persian temple. It was also said that it was only after a later Persian defeat by Rome that his skin was cremated and buried.

The humiliation of the Emperor Valerian by the Persian King Sapor by Hans Holbein (1498–1543) c. 1521. (Kunstmuseum Basel)

Diocletian (AD 244–311)

Diocletian—Gaius Aurelius Valerius Diocletianus Augustus—was born Diocles into a humble Dalmatian family and rose to become emperor from 284 to 305.

In an unsuccessful bid to eliminate Christianity from the empire he presided over the start of the Diocletianic Persecution (303–311), the empire's last, largest, and bloodiest official persecution of Christians. Before that, however, there were other instances of religious persecution by Diocletian. Sometime around AD 299, the four co-emperors Diocletian, Maximian, Flavius Constantius and Galerius participated in a traditional ceremony of sacrifice and divination in a bid to predict the future. The *haruspices* failed to read the entrails of the sacrificed animals: Christians in the imperial household were scapegoated The emperors also ordered all members of the court to perform a sacrifice to purify the palace and sent letters to the military, demanding the entire army perform the required sacrifices or face discharge.

Then, after some public disputes with Manicheans—a major religious movement founded by the Iranian prophet Mani—Diocletian ordered that the leading disciples of Mani be burned alive with their scriptures. In 302 he declared that low-status Manicheans be executed by the blade, and high-status Manicheans be sent to toil in the quarries of Proconnesus (modern-day Marmara Island in Turkey) or the mines of Phaeno in southern Palestine. All Manichean property was to be seized and deposited in the imperial treasury. The religiously conservative Diocletian was much offended by Manichean religion: he disliked its novelty, its foreignness, the way it corrupted the morals of the Roman race, and its inherent opposition to long-standing religious traditions.

When Diocletian returned to Antioch in 302, he ordered that the deacon Romanus of Caesarea have his tongue removed for arrogantly defying the order of the courts and interrupting official sacrifices. Romanus was then imprisoned and executed in November 303. According to Lactantius, Diocletian and co-emperor Galerius argued over imperial policy towards Christians, Diocletian arguing that barring Christians from the state bureaucracy and from the military would be enough to appease the gods, but Galerius pushed for extermination. The two men then sought the advice of the oracle of Apollo at Didyma. The oracle responded that the impious on Earth hindered Apollo's ability to provide advice. These 'impious ones', Diocletian was informed by members of the court, could only be Christians; Diocletian then gave in to demands for wholesale persecution. He ordered that the newly built Christian church at Nicomedia in Bythinia be razed to the ground and that its scriptures be burned; he seized its treasures for his treasury. The 20,000 Martyrs of Nicomedia, as the atrocity came to be known, marked a high point in the monstrous behaviour of Diocletian.

The atrocity took place after co-emperor Maximian (284–305) had returned victorious over the Ethiopians in AD 303. When Christians refused to sacrifice to

The 20,000 martyrs of Nicomedia. (http://days.pravoslavie.ru/Images/ii6938&3911.htm)

idols during Christmas Mass to thank the gods for the victory, Maximian and his troops entered the church and told the Christians they could escape punishment if they renounced Christ. The Christian priest Glycerius answered that the Christians would never renounce their faith, even under the threat of torture. Maximian ordered he be burned to death along with the congregation. Many were strangled or beheaded beforehand and the doors were locked from the outside. Those not burned in the church were rounded up and tortured to death. The bishop Anthimos who had escaped burning in the church was beheaded. While the number 20,000 may be an exaggeration, the martyrs of Nicomedia are still honoured with feast days: they are commemorated on 28 December in the Eastern Orthodox Church, and by the Byzantine Catholic and Latin Rite Catholic Churches.

The next day saw publication of Diocletian's first 'Edict against the Christians', ordering the destruction of Christian scriptures and places of worship across the empire, and prohibiting Christians from assembling for worship. When, at the end of February 304, a fire destroyed part of the imperial palace, Galerius persuaded Diocletian that the Christians were to blame, conspirators who had plotted with the eunuchs in the palace. Although an investigation drew a blank, executions followed

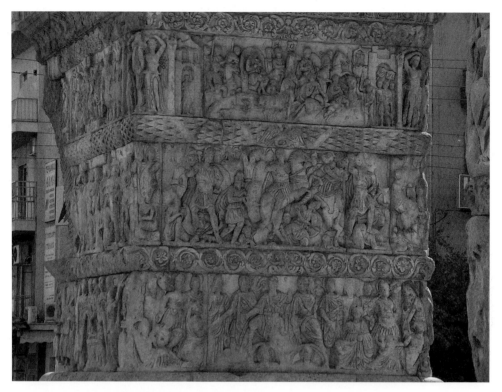

The Arch of Galerius, Thessaloniki.

regardless, and the palace eunuchs Dorotheus and Gorgonius were slain. Another victim, Peter Cubicularius, was stripped and scourged. Salt and vinegar were sprinkled in his wounds, and he was slowly boiled over an open fire. There was a second fire sixteen days after the first. Galerius left the city for Rome, declaring Nicomedia unsafe. Diocletian followed soon after.

For the record, Galerius's death in 311 was described as "shameful" and marked the end of a "life which his cruelty and sexual incontinence had made detestable". This death was shameful because "he was smitten with a most horrible disease in the most sensitive parts of his body, being devoured alive by maggots, and such a stench came from him that was offensive to those in the palace". It is thought to have been either bowel cancer, gangrene or Fournier gangrene.[*]

Febronia of Nisibis was a Christian nun at Nisibis in Mesopotamia. She was persecuted under Diocletian, who offered her freedom if she renounced her faith and married his nephew, Lysimachus, who had been showing tendencies towards

---

[*] Eusebius, *Historia Ecclesiae* 352–356; Lactantius, *De Mortibus Persecutorum* 33.

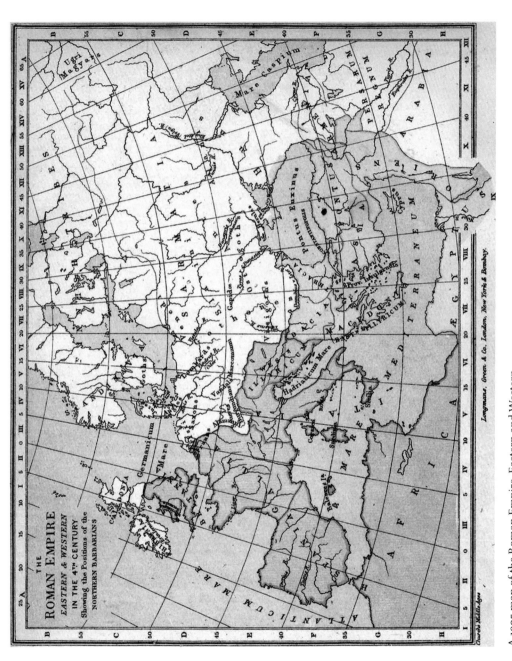

A 1905 map of the Roman Empire, Eastern and Western.

a conversion to Christianity. Febronia refused and was tortured; her breasts were cut off before she died. Lysimachus saw her suffering and proceeded with his conversion.

In the end, despite arrests of the Christian clergy, the edicts were unsuccessful; most Christians escaped punishment, and pagans had little interest in persecution. The martyrs' sufferings only strengthened the resolve of their fellow Christians while Constantius and Maximian did not apply the later edicts, leaving the Christians of the West unmolested. Within twenty-five years of the start of the persecution, there would be a Christian emperor on the throne in Constantine. He reversed the edicts, and returned all confiscated property to the Christians.

Justinian (c. AD 482–565)

Justinian I, Flavius Petrus Sabbatius Iustinianus Augustus, usually known as Justinian the Great, was the Eastern Roman emperor from 527 to 565. Justinian had ambitions to revive the empire's greatness and reconquer the lost western half of the historical Roman Empire—*renovatio imperii*.

However, his plans nearly came to nothing when in AD 532 Justinian faced a popular challenge to his leadership which escalated beyond all belief and culminated in the brutal extermination of 30,000 or so citizens of Constantinople, leaving much of the city in ruins.

What became known as the Nika riots started as a minor disturbance between rival factions at a chariot race in the Hippodrome. Fuelled by simmering political unrest, supporters of the Green and Blue factions clashed, destroying public buildings. The Hippodrome of Constantinople had lately become a cauldron of political dissent, so much so that the two usually irreconcilable factions came together in opposition to the government, initially demanding clemency for two of their members under sentence of death. Justinian, who had always been a Blues supporter, clumsily exacerbated the unrest with his impartiality. The turmoil graduated into a demand for Justinian to stand down. Initially he was set on deserting his capital but his wife, Theodora, was made of sterner stuff and persuaded him to stay and put down the riot by force.

Procopius describes the fierce rivalry in which the factions assume a political status running gangs and becoming the sole focus and mouthpiece for the social, religious and political issues of the day: "The population in every city has for a long been divided into two groups, the Greens and the Blues ... the members [of each faction] fight with their opponents ... respecting neither marriage nor kinship nor bonds of friendship, even if those who support different colours might be brothers or some other kind of relatives."

Mosaic of Justinian I.
(Sant'Apoilinare
Nuovo, Ravenna/
José Luiz Bernardes
Ribeiro)

Justinian's rule was characterized by heavy taxation levied to pay for his wars, by his despised administrators like John the Cappadocian and Tribonian, and by the move towards autonomy which alienated the Senate—all conspired to form a toxic cocktail of revolution centred on the Hippodrome. More heavy-handed policing in the weeks before the riots also served to inflame the simmering situation. Constantinople's Prefect Eudaemon made arrests: his inquiry found seven rioters guilty of murder and sentenced them to death. On execution day the hangman blundered and two of the men, a Green and a Blue, escaped and took sanctuary in the Church of St. Laurentius. Eudaemon dispatched soldiers to surround the church and during the next race meeting the factions came together. Procopius records that by the twenty-second race

JUSTINIAN is one of history's most notable homophobes. To Justinian the "man-woman" or effeminate male was disgusting; they "do unspeakable things" and "practise this sort of degradation" (*Apology* 1, 27, 2). In the 3rd century AD the Christian Marcus Julius Philippus (Philip the Arab, r. 244 to 249) had banned male prostitution. By the end of the 4th century, passive homosexuality (where a man was penetrated as opposed to penetrating) was punishable by burning and the punishment for a "man coupling like a woman" was death by the sword under the *Theodosian Code* (9, 7, 3). Justinian criminalized all same-sex acts, passive or active; they were deemed "contrary to nature" and thus punishable by death.

someone called out: "'Long live the humane Greens and Blues!' ... now the watch-word of which the populace passed to one another was 'Nike' which meant 'conquer' ... Fire was applied to the city as if it had fallen under the hand of an enemy."

As the violence increased and the buildings burned, Justinian made some lame attempts to control the situation but the mob insisted that the prisoners be released. When Eudaemon did not respond the people took control, attacked the garrison and released the prisoners themselves. Their initial objective realized, the rioters demanded that three unpopular officials be dismissed: Tribonian, Eudaemon and John the Cappadocian were replaced but that did not end the violence as the disaffected senate was now controlling events in the background and the palace guards and other peacekeeping forces were wavering.

A small force of Goths was deployed, unsuccessfully, to quell the riots. A number of senators were dismissed only to defect to the rebels. After a pitched battle with the rioters who were by now championing Hypatius as emperor elect, the palace itself was now under threat. (Flavius Hypatius was the nephew of Emperor Anastasius I, who had ruled AD 491–518.)

Justinian had a stark choice—flee or fight; he preferred the former but as we have seen, Theodora persuaded him otherwise: "My opinion then is that the present time, above all others, is inopportune for flight ... consider whether it will not come about after you have been saved that you would gladly exchange that safety for death. For as for myself, I approve a certain ancient saying that royalty is a good burial-shroud."

Justinian was now intent on quelling the riot once and for all. Narses, a loyal eunuch, was sent into the enemy camp to sow discord among the rioters, using bribes to remind the Blues of their rivalry with the Greens and of their former support of the emperor. Next, Belisarius and Mundus moved into the Hippodrome with a crack unit of soldiers and brutally attacked the rioters, who offered little resistance. Procopius gives the number of deaths as thirty thousand. Possibly an exaggeration but perhaps not when we remember that the Hippodrome is over four hundred metres long and can seat 30,000 people in its stands alone. Moreover, the population of Constantinople at the time was estimated at somewhere between 160,000 and 192,000. Justinian had Hypatius executed and exiled the senators who had supported the riot. He then rebuilt Constantinople and the Hagia Sophia, and was now free to pursue his ambition of presiding over a united Roman Empire.

Theodora (c. AD 500–548)

"Since mankind began there has never been such fear of any tyrant, for there was not even a possibility of concealment for one who had given offence. For a throng of spies kept reporting to her what was said and done both in the market-place and in the homes of the people."

Procopius

Theodora, the wife of Justinian I and powerful empress of the Byzantine empire, acted as a virtual co-regent with her husband. Procopius is our main source for her life, but perplexingly we have three wildly varying accounts from him in three separate works. *The Wars of Justinian* is complimentary and describes a brave and influential empress; Procopius's *De Aedificiis, Buildings of Justinian*, is a panegyric which shows Justinian and Theodora as a pious couple. But it is his *Anekdota* (unpublished works) or *Secret History*, published a thousand years later, which is of interest to us (the considerable delay in publication suggests that Procopius never intended this work to be published). When he wrote it, Procopius was disenchanted, depicting Justinian as cruel, greedy, wasteful and generally useless. As for Theodora, Procopius describes a woman who is vulgar and characterized by unquenchable lust—quite unrecognizable from his portrayals of her in the earlier works. To Procopius the couple are demons with disembodied heads that float around the palace by night. He nevertheless concedes that Theodora was not unattractive, if a little short and wan in complexion.

Corroboration of a kind comes from the Syriac historian John of Ephesus, when he describes Theodora as "coming from the brothel". Apparently, she was something of an authority on different types of abortion, having disposed of any number of unwanted and unintentional children Theodora's mother was an actress and a dancer; her father, Acacius, was a bear trainer at the Hippodrome in Constantinople. This marked the family out as *untermenschen*, socially equivalent to adulterers and prostitutes. John of Ephesus and Procopius concur that when she was young Theodora from an early age

Theodora, mosaic from the Basilica San Vitale, Ravenna.

followed her sister, Comito, who was something of a star, into work in a Constantinople brothel and later became an actress performing mime and obscene burlesque. One of her star roles was as Leda in a stage production of *Leda and the Swan*; this involved performing almost in the nude (total nudity was banned), and lying on her back while other actors scattered barley on her groin. The barley was then picked up by geese (as Zeus) with their beaks. Inviting fellow actors to copulate with her on stage was another party piece. Procopius relates with some distaste that in the early days Theodora was still too young to provide routine sexual intercourse but prostituted herself as a young boy, offering anal sex to her clientele, which included slaves.

In time she became a low-rent whore, one of "the dregs of the army", stripping off at the drop of a hat. Perfecting "novel ways of intercourse" was a specialty, as was her

The Empress Theodora
at the Colosseum
by Jean-Joseph
Benjamin-Constant
(1845–1902).
(Art Renewal
Center Museum)

enthusiastic participation in group sex at dinner parties. Ten or more young men in succession were easily accommodated; once these had been exhausted she moved on to their slaves, up to thirty at a time. Still her lust remained insatiable. She would often stand up in front of guests and lift up her dress to reveal her genitalia, complaining that Nature had only given her three orifices and that the holes in her nipples should be larger so that she could "devise another variety of intercourse in that region". According to Procopius, "with such lasciviousness did she misuse her own body that she appeared to have her private parts not like other women in the place intended by nature, but in her face."

After travelling around the Mediterranean from the age of sixteen, taking in Libya, Alexandria and Antioch, she returned to Constantinople in AD 522. In Libya she consorted with a certain Hecobolus "in order to serve him in the most revolting capacity". In Antioch she met a famous ballet dancer, Macedonia, whose day job was informer to Justinian. Procopius tells how Theodora apparently told Macedonia about a dream she had in which she would come back to Constantinople where the Lord of the Demons would seduce her, marry her and give her limitless riches.

The reality was not quite so glamorous. Arriving back in Constantinople, she renounced her former libidinous lifestyle and took on rather more matronly work as a wool spinner in a house near the imperial palace. By this time she had converted to Monophysitism, a non-orthodox Christian doctrine.* Her alleged beauty, wit and amiable ways attracted Justinian, then heir to the throne of his uncle, Emperor Justin I. Annoyingly for Justinian, Roman law prohibited government officials from marrying actresses, a law which Empress Euphemia fully supported. Justin had bought Euphemia as a slave when she was called Lupicina, with its overtones of *lupa* (she-wolf) suggesting that she was also a prostitute, adopting the respectable name of Euphemia when she became empress. However, Justin repealed the inconvenient law in 525 after Euphemia died, allowing Justinian to marry Theodora and to adopt Theodora's illegitimate daughter. The law erased Theodora's past reputation and restored her *pudicitia*, her chastity—a *damnatio memoriae* in reverse.

Erasure of a more sinister kind followed when Theodora's alleged affair with her slave Areobindus was discovered; she had him flogged and he disappeared from the scene. Procopius is quite incredulous that such a woman could rise from the lowest and most depraved of backgrounds to become empress of Rome. Justinian had the pick of all the women in his empire and could have selected "for his bride the most nobly born woman in the world ... thoroughly acquainted with the claims of modesty, and had lived in an atmosphere of chastity ... and still a virgin—or, as they say, firm-breasted"; instead he chose to "consort with a woman double-dyed with every kind of horrible pollution and guilty over and over again of infanticide by wilful abortion."

Procopius suggests that it was sheer lust which attracted Justinian to Theodora, but it seems that there was more to it than that. Theodora was desperate for another child and when the archimandrite (a celibate priest, one below a bishop) Mar Saba† visited Constantinople in 531 she pleaded with him that she might conceive; he insensitively refused, dashing her hopes when he declared that any son she bore would be a greater disaster for the empire than the Monophysite emperor Anastasius. Theodora never did conceive. After acquitting herself brilliantly, but ruthlessly, during the Nika riots in 532 by urging her dithering husband (now emperor) with a stirring speech

---

* A monophysite, in Christianity, believed that Jesus Christ's nature remains altogether divine and not human even though he has taken on an earthly and human body with its cycle of birth, life, and death.

† A famous Greek Orthodox monastery is named after Mar Saba, east of Bethlehem. Women have never been allowed in, even to this day, so female visitors have to make do with a glimpse from a nearby two-storey tower, the Women's Tower.

to stand and fight the rebels instead of fleeing, she, according to Procopius, grew excessively haughty. Court protocol was an obsession, with the relationship between emperor-empress and senators and others reduced to humiliation—something approaching master and slave: "They were kept waiting in a small, stuffy room for an endless time. After many days, some of them might at last be summoned, but going into her presence in great fear, they very quickly departed. They simply showed their respect by lying face down and touching the instep of each of her feet with their lips; there was no opportunity to speak or to make any request unless she told them to do so. The government officials had sunk into a slavish condition, and she was their slave-instructor."

Gibbon's assessment is something of a backhanded compliment, and a swipe at Procopius and his followers: "Those who believe that the female mind is totally depraved by the loss of chastity, will eagerly listen to all the invectives of private envy or popular resentment, which have dissembled the virtues of Theodora, exaggerated her vices, and condemned with rigour the venal and voluntary sins of the youthful harlot."

Her cruelty knew no bounds. Floggings stripped the flesh from victims' bones. One man was subjected to confinement in a manger with a noose around his neck so tight that he was unable to move; he was held like that in the dark for four months and was forced to eat, sleep and perform all bodily functions in that position. He died soon after release, quite insane and believing that he was a donkey. When a man called Vasianus insulted her she forced on him an "unendurable form of punishment"; pleas for mercy only intensified the torture and ended with his penis being cut off. When she turned against a man called Diogenes she had a strap of leather tied so tightly round his head that he felt that his eyes were about to burst out their sockets.

Nevertheless, despite the reputation—real or exaggerated—Theodora never forgot her roots and the prejudice she had suffered as a young girl; her work for women's rights was extensive and commendable. She championed laws prohibiting forced prostitution and closed down brothels. She established a convent on the Dardanelles called the Metanoia (Repentance), a kind of refuge where ex-prostitutes could be rehabilitated and support themselves. She also extended the rights of women in divorce and property ownership, equating a woman's rights here to a man's, brought in the death penalty for rape, banned the exposure of unwanted babies (usually girls), gave mothers some rights of guardianship over their children, criminalized the killing of a wife who committed adultery and legislated that a lover must receive three witnessed written warnings before he could be killed with impunity. A woman could no longer be imprisoned where she might be raped by male guards; if she had to be locked up then she should be sent to a convent. The ante-nuptial donation, a counter-dowry given by the husband to his wife, should be equal in value to the dowry.

A reading of the *Secret History* gives a very different picture of the woman: here Theodora is said to have rounded up 500 prostitutes, incarcerating them in a convent and leading to suicides as they tried to escape "the unwelcome transformation to a life of chastity". According to Victor of Tunnuna, Theodora died of what was probably breast cancer in 548, aged forty-eight. Justinian was distraught.

ANTONINA, married to Flavius Belisarius (c. AD 505–65), is bluntly summed up by Procopius: "Both her father and grandfather were charioteers, and her mother was one of the prostitutes attached to the theatre ... [Antonina] having in her early years lived a lewd sort of a life and having become dissolute in character, not only having consorted much with the cheap sorcerers who surrounded her parents, but also having thus acquired the knowledge of what she needed to know, later became the wedded wife of Belisarius, after having already been the mother of many children."

Belisarius was a successful general and faithful supporter of Justinian. He was largely responsible for suppressing the Nika riots with the massacre of 30,000 rebels in the Hippodrome at Constantinople. Procopius served as his secretary and advisor between AD 527 and 540. The duplicitous Antonina, brought with her a reputation even worse than Theodora's, and was alleged to have had an affair with her adopted son, Theodosius. Sex often took place in front of the slaves with Antonina "a slave to her lust"; even when Belisarius caught them in the act he was unwilling to believe what he had seen with his own eyes. Eventually though, the cuckolded Belisarius arrested Antonina on evidence provided by bedchamber servants but was unable to bring himself to exact punishment—due, according to Procopius, to Antonina's skilful use of the black arts. The informants were deemed to be lying: Antonina had their tongues cut out and their bodies chopped up; the body parts were dumped in the sea.

Justinian, however, is then said to have ordered Belisarius's eyes to be put out, and reduced him to the status of homeless beggar near the Pincian Gate of Rome, condemned to asking passersby to "give an obolus [a coin] to Belisarius" (*date obolum Belisario*), before pardoning him.

Theodora and Antonina were long-standing friends. Antonina was a schemer and a fixer of the first order, playing a prominent role in the downfalls of Pope

---

Belisarius begging for alms, as depicted in popular legend, in the painting by Jacques-Louis David (1781). (Palais des Beaux-Arts de Lille)

Byzantine mosaic depicting Empress Theodora flanked by a chaplain and a lady of court, believed to be her confidante Antonina, wife of the general Belisarius. (Basilica of San Vitale)

Silverius and John the Cappadocian, "making Silverius appear a pro-Gothic traitor" and implicating John "in a conspiracy to gain the throne". Theodora eventually restored Theodosius to a grateful Antonina, but not before she had whipped Photius, her son, half to death for concealing him. Theodosius died soon after of dysentery.

APPENDIX 1: THE REIGNS

Augustus (31 BCE–14 CE)
Tiberius (14–37 CE)
Caligula (37–41 CE)
Claudius (41–54 CE)
Nero (54–68 CE)
Galba (68–69 CE)
Otho (January–April 69 CE)
Aulus Vitellius (July–December 69 CE)
Vespasian (69–79 CE)
Titus (79–81 CE)
Domitian (81–96 CE)
Nerva (96–98 CE)
Trajan (98–117 CE)
Hadrian (117–138 CE)
Antoninus Pius (138–161 CE)
Marcus Aurelius (161–180 CE)
Lucius Verus (161–169 CE)
Commodus (177–192 CE)
Publius Helvius Pertinax (January–March 193 CE)
Marcus Didius Severus Julianus (March–June 193 CE)
Septimius Severus (193–211 CE)
Caracalla (198–217 CE)
Publius Septimius Geta (209–211 CE)
Macrinus (217–218 CE)
Elagabalus (218–222 CE)
Severus Alexander (222–235 CE)
Maximinus (235–238 CE)
Gordian I (March–April 238 CE)
Gordian II (March–April 238 CE)
Pupienus Maximus (April 22–July 29, 238 CE)
Balbinus (April 22–July 29, 238 CE)
Gordian III (238–244 CE)
Philip (244–249 CE)

Decius (249–251 CE)
Hostilian (251 CE)
Gallus (251–253 CE)
Aemilian (253 CE)
Valerian (253–260 CE)
Gallienus (253–268 CE)
Claudius II Gothicus (268–270 CE)
Quintillus (270 CE)
Aurelian (270–275 CE)
Tacitus (275–276 CE)
Florian (June–September 276 CE)
Probus (276–282 CE)
Carus (282–283 CE)
Numerian (283–284 CE)
Carinus (283–285 CE)
Diocletian (east, 284–305 CE; divided the empire into east and west)
Maximian (west, 286–305 CE)
Constantius I (west, 305–306 CE)
Galerius (east, 305–311 CE)
Severus (west, 306–307 CE)
Maxentius (west, 306–312 CE)
Constantine I (306–337 CE; reunified the empire)
Galerius Valerius Maximinus (310–313 CE)
Licinius (308–324 CE)
Constantine II (337–340 CE)
Constantius II (337–361 CE)
Constans I (337–350 CE)
Gallus Caesar (351–354 CE)
Julian (361–363 CE)
Jovian (363–364 CE)
Valentinian I (west, 364–375 CE)
Valens (east, 364–378 CE)
Gratian (west, 367–383 CE; co-emperor with Valentinian I)
Valentinian II (375–392 CE; crowned as child)
Theodosius I (east, 379–392 CE; east and west, 392–395 CE)
...
Justinian I (527–565 CE)
Theodora (c. 500–548 CE)

APPENDIX 2: THE JULIO-CLAUDIAN DYNASTY

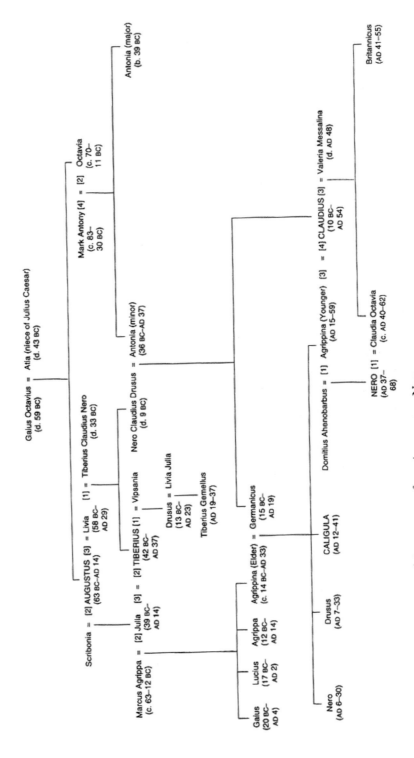

Simplified genealogical chart of the emperors from Augustus to Nero

APPENDIX 3: THE FLAVIAN DYNASTY

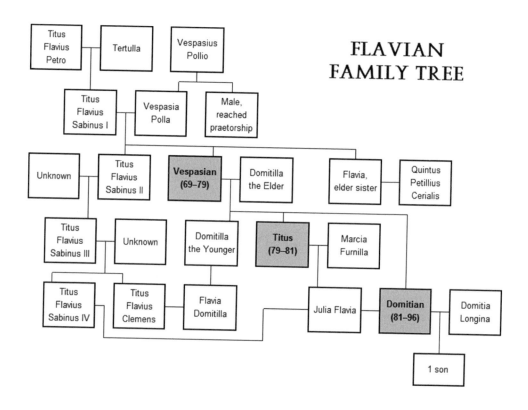

FLAVIAN
FAMILY TREE

FURTHER READING

In order to cover over five centuries of history, I have consulted, among many other contemporary sources, Flavius Josephus's *The Jewish War* and *Antiquities of the Jews*, Appian's *Mithridatic Wars* and *Bellum Civili*, Suetonius's *The Lives of the Twelve Caesars*, Plutarch's *Sulla*, Frontinus's *Strategemata*, Livy's *History of Rome*, Tacitus's *Annals*, Cassius Dio's *Roman History*, Julius Caesar's *De Bello Gallico*, Ambrosius Theodosius Macrobius's *Saturnalia*, Philo of Alexandria's *On the Embassy to Gaius*, Seneca's *Octavia* and *Dialogus*, Seneca the Younger's *On the Shortness of Life, On Firmness* and *On Anger*, Pliny, Juvenal, Eusebius's *Historia Ecclesiae*, Eutropius's *Breviarium Historiae Romanae*, Lactantius's *De Mortibus Persecutorum*, P. Herennius Dexippus, Procopius (several works) and last but not least *Historia Augusta*, or *The Augustan History*. The following modern publications also proved useful:

Adams, C., www.straightdope.com/columns/read/196/what-loathsome-disease-did-king-herod-die-of/ – 'Fighting ignorance since 1973. (It's taking longer than we thought)'

Adams, G. W., *The Emperor Commodus: Gladiator, Hercules or a Tyrant?*, Boca Raton, 2013

Adcock, F. E., *The Roman Art of War under the Republic*, via R. Beard, 2006

Baldwin, B., Executions under Claudius: Seneca's *Ludus de Morte Claudii*, Phoenix, 1964

_____, Nero and His Mother's Corpse: *Mnemosyne*, 1979

Barber, S., *Caligula: Divine Carnage: The Atrocities of the Roman Emperors*, New York, 2001

Barnes, T. D., 'Lactantius and Constantine', *Journal of Roman Studies* 63, 1973

_____, 'Legislation against the Christians', *Journal of Roman Studies* 58, 1968

_____, *Constantine and Eusebius*, Cambridge, 1981

Barrett, A. A., *Caligula: The Corruption of Power* 2nd ed., New Haven, 2015

Beard, M., 'Caligula was a sadistic, perverted megalomaniac—but he didn't eat his sister's baby', *Radio Times*, 29 July 2013

Bédoyère, Guy de la, *Domina: The Women Who Made Imperial Rome*, London, 2018

Benediktson, D. T., 'Caligula's Madness: Madness or Interictal Temporal Lobe Epilepsy?', *Classical World* 82, 1989

_____, 'Caligula's Phobias and Philias: Fear of Seizure?', *The Classical Journal* 87, 1991

Blond. A., *A Scandalous History of the Roman Emperors*, London, 2000

Boddington, A., 'Sejanus. Whose Conspiracy?', *American Journal of Philology* 84 1963

Boergas de Serviez, J., *Lives of the Roman Empresses*, London, 1935

Brauer, G. *The Decadent Emperors: Power and Depravity in Third-Century Rome* 2nd ed., London, 1995

Browning, R, *Justinian and Theodora* 2nd ed., London, 1987

Bury, J. B., *History of the Later Roman Empire Vol. II*, New York, 1958

Canduci, A., *Triumph and Tragedy: The Rise and Fall of Rome's Immortal Emperors.* Sydney, 2010

Cawthorn, N., *Sex Lives of the Roman Emperors*, London, 2008

Chrystal, P., *How to be a Roman*, Stroud, 2017

_____, *In Bed with the Romans,* Stroud, 2015

_____, *Roman Military Disasters*, Barnsley, 2015

_____, *Roman Record Keeping and Communications,* Stroud, 2018

_____, *Roman Women: The Women Who Influenced the History of Rome*, Stroud, 2015

_____, *Wars and Battles of the Roman Republic*, Stroud, 2015

_____, *When in Rome ... A Social History of Rome*, Stroud, 2017

_____, *Women at War in Ancient Greece & Rome,* Barnsley, 2017

_____, *Women in Ancient Rome*, Stroud, 2013

_____, *Rome: Republic into Empire,* Barnsley, 2019

Diehl, C., *Theodora, Empress of Byzantium,* New York, 1972

Digeser, E. D., *Lactantius and Rome: The Making of a Christian Empire*, Ithaca, 1999

Evans, J. A. S., *The Age of Justinian: The Circumstances of Imperial Power,*

Evans, J. A. S., *The Empress Theodora: Partner of Justinian*, Ann Arbor, 2003

Ferrill, A., *Caligula: Emperor of Rome.* New York, 1991

Garland, L., *Byzantine Empresses: Women and Power in Byzantium, AD 527–1204.* London, 1999

Gibbon, Edward, *The History of the Decline and Fall of the Roman Empire*, London, 1776–88

Gout, J., 'The Nike Revolt', *Encyclopædia Romana* http://penelope.uchicago.edu/~grout/ encyclopaedia_romana/circusmaximus/nike.html

Greatrex, G., 'The Nika Riot: A Reappraisal', *Journal of Hellenic Studies* 117, 1998

Griffin, M. T., *Nero: The End of a Dynasty*, London 2000

Holland, R., *Nero: The Man Behind the Myth,* Stroud, 2000

Holmes, W. G., *The Age of Justinian and Theodora Vols I & II*, London, 1912

Holum, K. K., *Theodosian Empresses: Women and Imperial Dominion in Late Antiquity,* Berkeley, 1982

Icks, M., *The Crimes of Elegabalus: The Life and Legacy of Rome's Decadent Boy Emperor,* London, 2011

Jones, B. W., *The Emperor Domitian*, London, 1992

Katz, R. S., 'The Illness of Caligula', *Classical World* 65, 1972

Keresztes, P., 'The Jews, the Christians, and Emperor Domitian', *Vigiliae Christianae* 27, 1973

Laiou, A. E. (ed.), *Consent and Coercion to Sex and Marriage in Ancient and Medieval Society.* Washington DC, 1993

Law, H. H., 'Atrocities in Greek Warfare', *Classical Journal* 15, 1919

McLynn, F., *Marcus Aurelius: A Life*, Boston MA, 2010

Montefiore, S. S., *Monsters: History's Most Evil Men and Women*, London, 2008

Morgan, M. G., 'Caligula's Illness Again', *Classical World* 66, 1973

Murison, C. L., 'Tiberius, Vitellius and the spintriae', *AHB* 1, 1987

Nagel, B. N., 'The Tyrant as Artist: Legal Fiction and Sexual Violence under

Pearn, J. H., Epilepsy and Drowning in Childhood', *British Medical Journal*, 1977

Rogers, R. S., 'The Conspiracy of Agrippina', *Transactions and Proceedings of the American Philological Association* 62, 1931

Salmon, E. T., *A History of the Roman World from 30 BC to AD 138*, London, 1983

Sandmel, S., *Herod: Profile of a Tyrant*, Philadelphia, 1967

Scott, A. G., *Cassius Dio, Caracalla and the Senate*, Berlin, 2015

Sidwell, B., 'Gaius Caligula's Mental Illness', *Classical World* 103, 2010

Syme, R., 'Seianus on the Aventine', *Hermes* 84, 1956

Temkin, O., *The Falling Sickness* 2nd ed., Baltimore, 1971

Turton, G., *The Syrian Princesses*, London, 1974

Vancea, S., *Justinian and the Nika Riots*, http://cliojournal.wikispaces.com/Justinian+and+the+nike+riots

Varner, E., *Mutilation and Transformation: Damnatio Memoriae and Roman Imperial Portraiture.* Leiden, 2004

Warner, D., 'Caligula and his Wives', *Latomus* 57, 1998

Wood, S., 'Caracalla and the French Revolution: A Roman Tyrant in Eighteenth-century Iconography', *Memoirs of the American Academy in Rome*, 2010

_____, 'Diva Drusilla Panthea and the Sisters of Caligula', *American Journal of Archaeology* 99, 1995

Woods, D., 'Nero and Sporus', *Latomus* 68, 2009

Zeitlin, S., 'Herod: A Malevolent Maniac', *Jewish Quarterly Review* 54, 1963

Index

Paul Chrystal has Classics degrees from the universities of Hull and Southampton; he is the author of around a hundred books, a number of which are on ancient history and literature. He writes for a national daily newspaper and has appeared on the BBC World Service Radio 4 PM programme and various BBC local radio stations. He is a regular contributor to Pen & Sword's the 'Military Legacy', 'History of Terror' and 'Cold War 1945–1991' series.

Also by Paul Chrystal

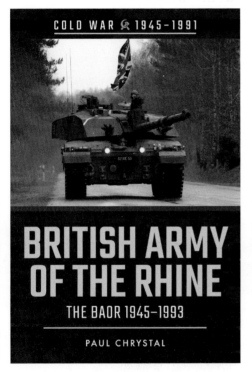

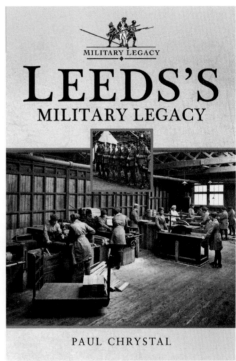

Other History of Terror Titles

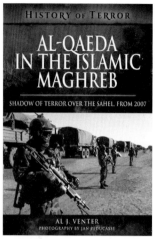

AL-QAEDA IN THE ISLAMIC MAGHREB

SHADOW OF TERROR OVER THE SAHEL, FROM 2007

AL J. VENTER
PHOTOGRAPHY BY JAN PEDUCASSE

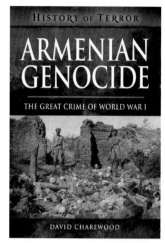

ARMENIAN GENOCIDE

THE GREAT CRIME OF WORLD WAR I

DAVID CHARLWOOD

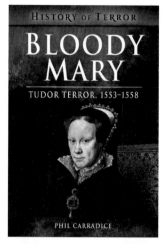

BLOODY MARY

TUDOR TERROR, 1553–1558

PHIL CARRADICE

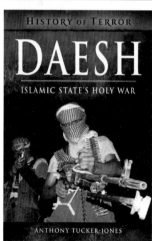

DAESH

ISLAMIC STATE'S HOLY WAR

ANTHONY TUCKER-JONES

NIGHT OF THE LONG KNIVES

HITLER'S EXCISION OF ROHM'S
SA BROWNSHIRTS, 30 JUNE–2 JULY 1934

PHIL CARRADICE

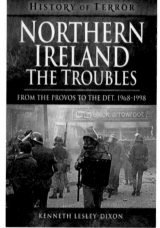

NORTHERN IRELAND THE TROUBLES

FROM THE PROVOS TO THE DET, 1968–1998

KENNETH LESLEY-DIXON

THE SHANGHAI MASSACRE

CHINA'S WHITE TERROR, 1927

PHIL CARRADICE

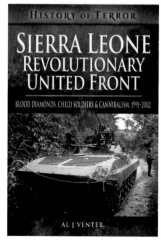

SIERRA LEONE REVOLUTIONARY UNITED FRONT

BLOOD DIAMONDS, CHILD SOLDIERS & CANNIBALISM, 1991–2002

AL J VENTER

SS EINSATZGRUPPEN

NAZI DEATH SQUADS, 1939–1945

GERRY VAN TONDER